F.A.M.E.

FLIGHT.ATTENDANT.MODEL.ENTREPRENEUR

Life

How I Walked Away, Took Flight and Built the Life I Deserve

WENDY NICOLE DAVIS

ISBN: 978-1-949430-11-0

Liberated Expression Publishing

Chicago, Illinois

Printed in the United States of America

Library of Congress Control Number: 2026940323

A Letter from the Author:

I am Wendy Nicole Davis and before this book existed—before the healing, before the rising—I lived through my own seasons of breaking, silence and awakening.

Some people first met me as "The Lady in the Blue Dress" on *The Steve Harvey Show*, but very few knew the pain, the confusion, the unraveling and the rebirth happening behind that smile.

Writing this book became a part of my healing.

A sacred reflection of everything I survived.

These pages hold the parts of me I once whispered only to myself—the truth of losing my voice, abandoning my needs, shrinking to be loved and the quiet courage it took to choose myself again.

My healing wasn't sudden. It was slow, spiritual and deeply personal. It happened in the small, holy moments where God, grace and my own spirit reminded me I was still worthy of peace.

I share this story because someone else needs to know that healing is possible.

That leaving can be sacred.

That softness is strength.

That you don't have to stay broken to be worthy of a beautiful life.

My hope is that as you read this book, you feel seen, you feel held and you feel permission to begin again— without shame, without rushing, without abandoning yourself.

Thank you for allowing me to share my heart with you.

Thank you for letting me walk beside you in these pages.

You matter.

Your healing matters.

And you can rise. Slowly. Gently. Powerfully.

Every day you choose yourself.

—**Wendy**

Dedication

For every woman who has carried storms in silence.
Who has broken and rebuilt herself in the dark.
Who has searched for her own light
in places that forgot her name.

May these pages be a soft landing.
A mirror.
A breath you didn't know you needed.
A reminder that your becoming
is holy work.

Table of Contents:

Introduction

Seven years.

Seven long, heavy years.

It was a mess—emotionally, financially, spiritually. But I'm not telling this story to be bitter. I'm telling it so that someone else knows what to look for before they sign up to be someone's emotional cosigner... or their credit cosigner.

For a long time, I thought I was destroying the life I had spent years carefully building. In reality, I was setting myself free.

Brian stood there in disbelief as he watched me—calm, focused and in motion—sorting through my life and separating it from his. He thought I was bluffing. He thought I just wanted attention. He thought I was trying to scare him.

But I was done talking.

It took years to reach that point—to rebuild just enough strength, dignity and self-respect to finally choose myself. And once I arrived there, nothing was pulling me back.

I'll never forget the conversation that snapped everything into place.

"Everyone thinks there is something spectacular about you," he said, "but there is nothing spectacular about you to *me*. And you feel that way about yourself. That's why you're doing all this... the modeling, acting, getting dressed up, taking pictures."

He walked across the room while I sat there watching him, my mouth open in disbelief. Instinctively—defensively—I said, "How about I get paid to do this?"

Immediately, I caught myself. That was the wrong response. That wasn't the woman I wanted to be. It was reactive. Emotional.

So I asked softly, "Then why am I here?" Louder the second time, "Why am I here then? Because clearly, I'm not wanted here."

I stood up from the couch—where moments earlier I had been watching myself on an episode of *Chicago Med*, so proud of that booking—and followed him as he walked into the bathroom.

Again, "Then why am I here?"

His reply is something I will never forget, "Sometimes we're in situations where we have to settle and don't have any other choice. This is the life we were given."

Settle? Who has to settle? Not me!!

I'm forty-one years old. Beautiful. Successful. Honest. Kind.

A good woman and a good person. I don't have to settle and I won't.

Before he could say another word, I cut him off.

"Don't worry about it. I'll be out of your way before the end of the month. I'm not staying somewhere I'm not wanted."

"Good. Leave," he said.

"I will," were my final words.

I'm not a woman who makes empty threats.

I mean what I say and I say what I mean.

It was the first week of November. My plan was to have everything packed, handled and closed out by the end of the next week. Two weeks to dismantle a seven-year life.

The apartment wasn't fancy—it was livable. A well-lit living room. A plush brown sectional we had separated into two parts—the chaise for me, the three-cushion side for him. A weight bench in the corner. A big ottoman. I had decorated my room, but never the apartment. I never felt comfortable enough to make it a home.

We moved in September 2019. Within two months, he brought another woman into the house—and while I was physically there, in my room, he fucked her.

Because we had separate bedrooms and because he liked the façade of "just roommates," it made it easy for him to justify whatever he wanted to do. He claimed that because my door was closed, I must've had another man in my room. That was the excuse he used to rationalize bringing her into our home.

She even left a bloody towel on my bathroom sink. And then he left too—stayed at her place for days, acting like I had done something wrong.

That apartment was never "home" again.

Weeks before he told me that there was nothing spectacular about me, every time he drank, I quietly packed a box and slid it deep into my closet. My soul had already started leaving long before my body did.

I had a lot to do in the short amount of time I gave myself. I had to close out bank accounts, settle personal and business matters, coordinate with the landlord to remove my name from the lease and clear out utility bills. I sold one of my Turo cars and surrendered my Slingshot back to the bank.

Survival mode doesn't even begin to describe it.

And while I was trying to exit peacefully, he started spinning lies—fast.

He told people I stole money from him.
That he gave me rent money and I pocketed it.
That I maxed out his cards.
That I ruined his credit.
That *I* was the problem.

Lies spread quickly, especially when the truth threatens someone's ego.

Bills were behind.
Accounts were closing or going to collections.
I sold what I could of *my* belongings.
Whatever I couldn't take, I walked away from.

He painted himself as the victim.
As if I had wronged him.
As if I had destroyed him.
As if I had been living off of him.

Seven years of chaos.
Seven years of distortion.
Seven years of shrinking myself to fit inside a life that was never meant for me. Even today, sometimes I catch myself thinking, *This couldn't have been my life.* But it was...

And this—this moment of clarity, truth and breaking—is where it all truly begins.

Let's get into it...

Chapter 1

Enough

"Heartbreak is the recognition that something you worked toward, prepared for or believed in has been taken away by circumstances beyond your control. It is the collapse of expectation into reality, marked by loss, interruption and the forced acceptance that effort alone does not guarantee outcome."

2022 came in like a thief—disruptive, cold and unrelenting. The world was still reeling from the grip of COVID and although we had made it through the worst years of the pandemic, the virus hadn't gone anywhere. I had done my best to stay safe. Extremely cautious, really. Running a notary business during a pandemic meant I had minimal direct contact with people and when I did, I was masked, gloved and carrying sanitizing spray like my life depended on it—because it did. I didn't take risks. I didn't tempt fate.

But one cold day, I slipped. I was managing my Turo business at the time and the weather was biting.

As I approached the vehicle to start the return process, I noticed that he had a slight limp when he exited the vehicle. He was an older black man, perhaps in his early sixties, gray hair and I could tell that he was in a bit of a hurry. He was wearing a red and black checkered shirt with blue jeans and a black leather jacket.

"Hi… how was everything?" I asked him as I walked up to him.

"I really enjoyed the car," he assured me and proceeded to inquire about working out a deal outside of the company for long-term rental arrangements.

I had to make sure I went through the return process, which included obtaining any feedback from the customers about any issues they may have had, checking the return mileage and gas levels and taking detailed pictures for any damages that occurred during their trip. The last step was to complete the final report, reconcile any additional fees they owed and provide a review. Due to the weather being below zero, I skipped the most important step—given the times we were in—I did not sanitize the car like I normally would have and instead, just hopped in, cranked the heat and rushed home. I told myself I'd be fine. I wasn't.

Days later, I was on set for a commercial—a healthcare company gig that was a major booking and scheduled to air during the Super Bowl. It was my first big job of the year. That alone made it special. I arrived ready and excited. Walking into the clinic, I noticed a mixture of actual patients, staff and talent in the waiting room. There were seven of us that were scheduled for the shoot. We waited patiently to be called to check in with the production crew, have our temperatures taken and fill out paperwork. We were called one by one to complete the preliminary process. Once completed, we were escorted to our holding room. There were ten round tables, three clothing racks with our wardrobe, three makeup artists, a hair stylist, a clothing stylist and the rest of the production crew. They offered us a light snack of fresh fruit, veggies and dip, sandwiches, a variety of sweets and beverages as we were getting settled in at our individual tables. Once settled, they gave the run-down of the evening as this was an evening shoot. The last order of business that needed to be taken care of, was completing rapid COVID tests depending on prior testing. Myself, along with three other talents were given tests and had to wait fifteen minutes before we could proceed with the evening depending on the results. I figured it was routine. What I didn't expect was the woman with the test telling me, "You're positive." She was an older white lady who appeared to be ten to fifteen years older than me. She wore a white t-shirt, blue jeans and her hair was in a short, blonde bob. The words echoed. "You're positive."

My first response was confusion.

"What are you talking about?" I asked. I didn't feel sick. I had no symptoms. "Please run the test again," I asked her, convinced it was a mistake.

She did. It wasn't. I was positive. And just like that, everything crumbled.

I stood there, heart in pieces, trying to hold back my tears, I couldn't. I watched my first big opportunity of the year vanish in front of me. The first thing I did was take out my cell phone.

"Hello Sarah, this is Wendy Davis. I'm at the healthcare company shoot." My voice quivered. "They ran the rapid COVID test and I tested positive." I was so disappointed with the situation.

"Thank you for letting me know," my agent replied. I could hear the disappointment in her voice. "I hope you feel better," she ended.

I pressed the end button on the call and sank into the reality of what was happening.

After the results were officially confirmed and I had called my agent to explain the situation, I was given time to pack up my belongings. They were making adjustments to the flow of the evening. Once I had everything together, the producer's assistant, a younger white lady who appeared to be ten to fifteen years younger than me, stepped in and asked if I wanted a hug. I did but I asked her, "aren't you worried?" She assured me she wasn't worried and gave me a tight, heartfelt hug. My spirits were shattered as I left the building, walked to and got in my car and drove out the parking lot. And as if on cue, now that I knew I had COVID, my body began to feel it. The symptoms rolled in like an unwanted wave. It was as if the confirmation gave the virus permission to surface.

When I got home, I began notifying everyone I had been around. Thankfully, only two people outside of my household had been in contact with me and they were both fine. The first call I made was to a client and friend that stopped by for about fifteen minutes to drop off some paperwork and to check out my new office.

"Hey," I said, exhaustedly. "I just tested positive for COVID, so you might want to get tested to make sure that you don't have it."

"Okay," he replied. He was quiet. He said he would get tested, but the way he brushed it off and was nonchalant bothered me more than I expected. Fortunately, he was negative.

The other person was more proactive. When I told him that I was just diagnosed with COVID and that he should get tested, he was unbothered and mentioned that he wasn't worried. At this point, I asked him what kind of immune system he had that made him not worried. He shared with me a list of recommended immune boosters and holistic remedies that he swore religiously about: oil of oregano, echinacea goldenseal and wild cherry bark tea.

I followed his advice religiously and surprisingly, it worked. Within a few days, I was feeling better, physically at least. Emotionally, I was still nursing the blow of what felt like a stolen opportunity.

Still, I got back to work.

I had a business conference in Atlanta that I couldn't afford to miss. I traveled, networked, took notes and when I came home, I was ready to dive back into the grind. I headed to my office, expecting a normal day of printing documents and preparing for client closings.

When I arrived, the block was lit up with flashing lights, fire trucks and the unmistakable smell of smoke. There were firefighters and police officers chaotically running up and down the street and in and out of the building, through the frame of the door where the glass was shattered from the impact of the fire. It still didn't quite hit me what was going on. All I was focused on was getting my documents printed so that I could get to work and go on about my day. My heart dropped. There had been an electrical fire in the building overnight. My office was gone.

It seemed like every time I'd take 2 steps forward, I would be thrown 10 steps back. Every time I would try to get ahead and make what would seem to be progress, it all would be taken away. This wasn't the first time I was in a situation where I lost everything I've worked for or at least it sure felt like it. All I knew was that I've felt this before and it didn't feel good.

In shock, I tried to process it. Once they cleared the scene and made sure it was safe, one of the firefighters escorted me through the building to my office, briefly to salvage what I could. As I stepped through the glass shattered doorway and walked up the damp, smoke stenched stairway, I was fearful of what I would see when I reached the top. I was met with a dark, flooded hallway, cork ceiling tiles blown out and hanging on for dear life. It smelled of burnt wood and mold. As I walked past each office, looking in to see what damage was caused to other businesses, my stomach began to feel queasy and my head started to hurt. Partially because of the smell but mostly because of the disappointment, anger and the feeling of defeat. When I approached my office, I grabbed my computer, a printer, some printer paper and a few other essentials. Everything else smelled of smoke, saturated in thick films of soot, displayed visible water damage or was lost in the chaos. Once I gathered what I needed, I was able to walk down the rest of the hallway to see what else the fire destroyed. All of our offices were beyond minor repairs. There were major flooding damages, electrical damages, personal property damages etc. I turned around and walked out shaken. I didn't have the strength, energy or heart to deal with it at the moment. I had spent time and love making that office peaceful and welcoming. I'd painted the walls a rich purple, decorated it with intention and set up a cozy environment for myself and my clients. It was my space— my escape. The reason I got the office in the first place was because home wasn't peaceful.

At home, I was always "too present." I was told I didn't know how to give a man space, that I didn't know how to be a woman in a relationship and that my constant presence was suffocating. So, I thought that by removing myself from the house more often—having a place of my own to work—would help.

It did, for a while.

Until it burned down.

Once I returned to my car, loaded up what I was able to retrieve from my office, I got in and carefully drove away from the scene. When I was finally calm, I called Brian. The conversation didn't go quite how I expected. I started the conversation off with, "you'll never guess what just happened". He seemed invested and attentive while I was giving him the details. I explained to him what the scene looked like when I pulled up, the interaction I had with the fire department, the process I had to go through getting my equipment and supplies, what my office and the rest of the building looked like, the damage that had been done and finally, how devastated and defeated I felt. Instead of offering comfort, support and love, I was faced with sarcasm and statements like, "I didn't want you to get the place anyway". "I didn't like that area anyway". "I'm glad this happened, you didn't need it anyway. It was a bad decision in the first place." I remember when I first told him I was looking and had found the perfect place, he didn't want to come to see it, didn't want to help me find people to help paint, get me settled, move my belongings in, nothing. I believe over the course of the eight months I had my office, he came two times and those times were forced. I was so proud and I wanted to show him my new space. The other time was him helping me move the things I was able to salvage after the fire.

What hurt more than losing the office was how he reacted. It wasn't disappointment. It wasn't concern. It was something else—like satisfaction. As if my loss meant something good for him. With the office gone, I had to move back into the house. He didn't say much, but the look in his eyes said everything.

I tried to make it work. I set my office back up in my room and would occasionally work at the dining room table for a change of scenery. In that same dining room space, I recorded auditions, created content and tried to maintain a professional environment in a personal space. But that was a problem too. "You just gon' turn the whole house into a studio now?" he said, annoyed. And yes, I did. Because this was my career. This was how I paid the bills—his and mine. Through all of his temper tantrums, I couldn't help but think… if he had something to do, he could stop worrying about what I was doing. If he had something going on that was positive and productive, he wouldn't be so concerned about my working and not paying him any attention...I think that was the real problem. As much as he complained and griped, he wasn't the center of attention and if he wasn't, then there was a problem with everything and everyone. In his sick and twisted mind, he felt he should have been a kept "Man" and since he "was" the man back in the day, he was entitled and earned the right to be taken care of. Sir...I didn't know you back then... I had lost all the respect I had for him a very long time ago.

I was still running my businesses, managing vehicle pickups and drop-offs through Turo, even though he offered no help unless his car was involved. I'd Uber to drop off or pick up vehicles—sometimes at night, alone—because he wouldn't assist unless there was something in it for him. Only when we added his car to the fleet did he begin to care.

Despite all that, business was going well. Modeling, acting and entrepreneurship were all picking up speed. And though the office fire had been devastating, the insurance settlements brought a silver lining. I had coverage for all five of my businesses. Three of the settlements were lump sums and the remaining two paid out monthly—about $4,000 to $5,000, which sustained me for a year. It was an unexpected relief.

I didn't let him know about the settlements. It was none of his business. He always looked at my business as "lil" and would often say, "you're treating them like they make you millions and millions of dollars," but these "lil" businesses were providing for the BOTH of us. Even though I had no Idea of how and when I was leaving, all I knew is that it had to happen. I looked at this as a blessing in disguise and an opportunity to build my nest egg and to start removing myself from commitments and obligations, so that I could leave peacefully, gracefully and with dignity.

When he saw a job opportunity at the post office, I helped him apply. I filled out paperwork, reviewed his emails and encouraged him the whole way. He got the job and everything seemed set. Initially, he was given a later start date, but due to payroll cycles, they needed him to start a week earlier. He agreed. We had a plan in place for rest, nourishment and sobering up. The first few days went well. I would prepare nutritious protein shakes and smoothies, prepare fresh juice and hearty meals. We would go out and get fresh air, walk around our neighborhood and beautiful park and do the one thing we both loved so much—sitting for hours listening to good music. That lasted for a few days. He was feeling better, resting and flushing his system. He seemed motivated, excited and looked at this as an opportunity for change and a fresh start. Things were good for a few days, except the cravings came back and were getting worse. He felt like if he kept drinking and drinking and drinking, he'd be fine. I tried to encourage him and keep him motivated and distracted, but there is only so much one can do, so I let him be and went on about my daily activities. You can't want more for someone than they want for themselves.

Then came the morning of orientation.

I had a shoot that same day for Chicago Med, so I got up early to make sure we didn't get in each other's way. I made coffee, cooked him breakfast consisting of a fried egg, salami and toast, packed a light lunch with flavored rice, summer sausage, bell peppers and onions, cucumbers on the side with accent and chips. Lunch was going to be provided for him, but he still wanted something just in case. I got myself ready with minimal effort. I just had to show up on set. He tried. He really did. But when it came time to get himself together, he said he couldn't do it. He wasn't feeling well. I told him there was still time to pull himself together, to rest a bit and try again. He did. But it didn't help. At that point we went back and forth discussing the opportunity and what he was risking by not going. Once again, that sense of entitlement kicked in. He felt like they owed him something, that they should wait on him to start the position the next week since that was what they originally presented him with and that he was actually too good for the position. Internally, I was sick and tired of the entitlement and audacity. You have no high school education, a convicted felon and an alcoholic. What leverage do you actually have? I was over everything "him" at this point.

Eventually, he asked me to email the recruiting team, as if I was him and let them know he wouldn't make it. I did. They responded, asking if he could at least start on the first workday in two days. He refused, saying he needed another week. And with that, the opportunity slipped away. In my mind, even if he couldn't attend the orientation those two days, if he could at least get started working, they would have him attend the orientation the following week. It seemed as if they were trying to work with him the best they could.

I was furious.

I went to my shoot, completed my work and checked in on him throughout the day. He was feeling better, of course. But the chance was gone. That day, I realized I could no longer keep living this way. Something had to change. I needed a plan.

I booked appointments with a therapist and a psychiatrist. I had been misdiagnosed with bipolar II disorder in the past, but after a proper evaluation, I was diagnosed with PTSD, C-

PTSD and ADHD. I had spent years functioning in survival mode, overcompensating, pushing through pain, lying, suffering and enduring extreme mental, emotional, financial, spiritual and narcissistic abuse. I agreed to try medication for ADHD—anything that could help quiet my mind so I could focus and heal. Therapy became my anchor. I went weekly. I looked forward to it. For the first time in a long time, I felt heard.

We worked on everything—boundaries, confidence, self-worth, emotional triggers. My therapist suggested a positivity journal to reframe how I saw myself. I had spent years journaling my pain, chronicling one traumatic event after another like a police report. I recently tore it all up. I didn't want to carry it anymore. That was my release.

But the facts were still clear: I had survived multiple evictions, three car repossessions and was carrying the financial weight for two people. He rarely contributed. If I asked for help, it became an ordeal—tantrums, guilt trips, stonewalling. Eventually, I stopped asking.

Then October came.

I traveled for my best friend's wedding—a needed break, a beautiful experience. When I returned, I walked into the house and was met with this:

"Everybody thinks there's something spectacular about you, but there's nothing spectacular about you to me and you feel that way about yourself."

He said it like a dagger. With intention.

He continued: "That's why you're doing all that modeling and acting, dressing up and taking pictures. You think you're somebody."

But I didn't just think—I knew. I had worked too hard to forget.

I Started Modeling and Acting professionally when I was sixteen. I was very shy and reserved and that was my creative outlet. My time to be in the spotlight with minimal effort. It came naturally to me. I worked hard to get to the level that I was at that time. The recognition, respect and being in demand was priceless. So yes, I knew! He was jealous of me. He always looked at me as competition instead of us being a team. He would often tell me that it was time to give it up and who was I trying to prove something to or impress. That was one of the biggest mistakes he could have ever made... trying to crush my dream and devalue my accomplishments and goals. Now that I think about it, he never really liked me as a person. He liked the idea of me and what all was attached to me.

I looked at him and asked, "Then why am I here? If you don't see value in me, why should I stay?"

He had no real answer. Only weak excuses about people being "stuck" and having to "settle." That was it for me.

I told him I'd be out by the end of the month. And I meant it.

That week, I started shutting everything down—closed bank accounts, notified clients, sold off equipment, ended leases. I told the bank to come get their vehicle or they'd never find it. I sold one of my cars to CarMax and kept only what I needed to survive.

It was time. Not just to escape—but to be free

We Are Not the Same

You wanted to be something and someone you weren't. You wanted to be me. You envied how I moved around with so much grace and class. You envied how much of an influence I had on people. You envied the way people looked at me with respect and admiration. But we are not the same. I operate from a place of integrity, kindness and love. You on the other hand, from a place of manipulation, deceit and lies. I played your game for a while. I lied to make you seem like this standup guy. I lied so you could appear to be the big man in charge. I lied so you could appear to want more for yourself than you actually did. But we are not the same. I stroked your ego. I co-signed on this past version of yourself that you just couldn't let go of. You were always in competition with me when we should have been a team. You always tried to make me feel and look as if I was beneath you. But we are not the same. See, the thing is, I wanted more for you than you wanted for yourself. I saw this illusion of potential that wasn't there. I fooled myself. I was looking for something in you, when it was within myself all along. But we are not the same. I wanted to see you overcome your demons. I wanted to see you become the best version of yourself, while you were plotting my downfall. You were getting people to turn on me with your lies and manipulation and playing the victim... Joke's on you because... We... are not... the same.

Chapter 2

Theeee Audacity

"The audacity of a narcissist is the calculated entitlement to control, deceive and violate others while presuming immunity from consequence. It is audacity operationalized— the deliberate distortion of reality, routine boundary violations and infliction of harm paired with the expectation of silence, compliance or absolution. This conduct is sustained through denial, minimization and deflection, not misunderstanding. Its defining feature is the presumption that the injured party will doubt themselves, accommodate the abuse and tolerate what was never justified."

I remember when I first stumbled upon that apartment—it was completely by accident. I had just come out of a long stretch living in a basement apartment, surrounded by people who introduced me to Buddhism. That space had served its purpose, but I was ready for something more. A peaceful, brighter space. Something that didn't feel like I was hiding.

I was actually driving around one day, lost while looking for a different property. That's when I saw a "For Rent" sign tucked into the front lawn of a brick walk-up. Something about it called to me. I pulled over and dialed the number listed. A woman answered, kind and direct. "I'm not there now," she said, "but I can be there in about thirty minutes."

Perfect.

While I waited, I drove around the neighborhood to get a feel for it. It was quiet, peaceful. The kind of area where kids could ride their bikes and nobody worried too much. There was a park just a few blocks away. A grocery store within walking distance and everything I needed nearby. It felt like a real community. Not too far in the city to feel congested, but close enough that Brian wouldn't complain about the drive. That mattered back then—for some reason.

When I pulled back up to the building, I was still early for our meeting. I sat in my car reflecting over the yeara of our various living situations. I moved back from LA to Chicago when my lease was up. I was in LA for about 6 months pursuing my dream of modeling and acting. I was doing well.

I was building a foundation, network and booking work. When I left for LA earlier that year, I rented my two-bedroom, one bath, eleventh floor, luxury condo to a "friend" and his girlfriend. It was supposed to be a win-win situation. They would stay there, their payments would cover the mortgage and assessments, while I was laying the foundation for my new life. I was excited. That was one less thing I had to worry about and I trusted them.

Mark was an older man. He was like one of those older uncle type figures. He was the maintenance man at a different condo I owned a few years prior to me owning the one I rented to them. When I lost everything, due to several unfortunate real estate investments, he vouched for me with the owner of another complex he worked at and I was able to rent an apartment and start rebuilding. So, we had history to say the least.

I was not trying to make a profit; I just wanted my payments to be taken care of. That situation became very messy and I had to end up evicting them. My consistent trips to and from Chicago became exhausting and I made the decision when my lease was up to come back, wrap everything up, sell my place and go back to LA. Unfortunately, it was not that simple. I went through months of going to court, the eviction process and being threatened. I felt like I needed to be close to take care of my business. When I got back to Chicago, I did not have a stable place to stay, as they were in my place.

We met at a birthday party, hit it off and moved in together immediately. We were staying at a family house. My intentions were still to sell my place, wrap everything up and go back to LA...possibly with him. When I finally was able to get the tenants out of my condo, it was taking a very long time to sell my place. I moved back in until it sold. I did invite him to come, but he refused, as he wanted to stay in the hood where all the action was. He resented me every time I would have him visit and immediately wanted to go home. This is where I start trying to accommodate him with the living situations.

I was finally able to sell my place a year later and at that time life was "lifeing..." there was no going back to LA at this time. Closer to where he currently was but not too far away from what I needed and my comfortability level, I rented a two bedroom, one bathroom apartment on the Northside of Chicago. It was nice. I had enough room to have a dedicated office, nice hardwood floors, amazing windows that let in a lot of natural light, two dedicated parking spots, with a washer and dryer in the unit.

He didn't move in initially. I asked a few times and at some point, I stopped. I made the place home and comfortable for me. When he decided he was ready to come, I welcomed him with open arms. It was good for a while and then the complaints came about me not having a room for him or extra space for him of his own... HUH?" Well, Sir, you weren't coming, remember..."that situation lasted until he got laid off from his job for the winter season. It was like pulling teeth to get him to help me with the bills and basic expenses. He was not eligible for unemployment since he hadn't had enough work history under his belt. His car payment fell behind. One of "his" child's mother's was trying so hard to get him to be active in her life.

In the past he was reluctant because he was not sure the child was his... However, he took this time as an opportunity to start showing up more... he would go and come back and finally when she offered to pay the car note if she could use it, he felt that at the perfect opportunity to leave me and go out there with her because she could take care of that and him. At this point I was depleted and going in the hole trying to take care of the both of us. He moved out like a thief in the night with a few Walmart plastic grocery bags.

Needless to say this was the beginning of a continuous eviction cycle. It got to the point where I fell behind and could not redeem myself. My landlord worked with me as much as he could but I didn't want an eviction on my record so we agreed, I would leave before it got to that point. I asked Brian for help, I asked people who owed me money for help, I did UberEats until I got sick, vision got blurry and I hit the side of a car. I gave up at that point. Fortunately, I was able to secure an apartment and move in. It was a one bedroom, one bathroom... AND AGAIN, he was not initially moving with me as he had left me for this other woman.

I was able to move in, get settled and create a healthy space. At some point, it didn't work out between them. She pulled a gun out on him and started stalking me. He had to steal his car back and once again, I welcomed him with open arms. No job, income. Nothing... just him.

Eventually I got evicted from this place as well. Taking care of two adults with no help. I believe this was during the time his job called him back to work for the season. He had worked one season at her house and now starting another season with me. I was blessed to be offered the basement apartment at one of my Buddhists member's buildings. At this point, he went back out to her house to get his things and stayed because she fell severely ill... (who knows the truth in that). I got settled in. AGAIN, a two-bedroom, one bathroom space. I made the second bedroom my office. AGAIN, he comes with the same complaint about me not having space for him. Sir... I didn't know you were coming.

After she "recovered," he came to live with me in the basement apartment. It was dark, depressing, damp, but it was what I had to work with at the moment. We stayed in that space for ten months until I decided it was time to come out of that depressing situation.

When I met the landlord, she gave me a tour. It was a two-bedroom, one-bath unit on the third floor of a six-unit building. The layout was simple, but it felt fresh. One bedroom had a walk-in closet and a small balcony. The other was smaller but functional. The kitchen had been updated, modern countertops, stainless steel appliances. A dedicated dining space flowed into a cozy living room with great light. It was the kind of place I could breathe in.

I took it.

At the time, my credit wasn't perfect, but she gave me a chance. I signed the paperwork and moved in with a mixture of hope and hesitation. Two parking spaces came with the lease. Later, when we got the Slingshot, she let me rent the garage. That's also where I stored a few things I didn't have space for inside. Thankfully, the laundry area had a storage closet.

It wasn't just an apartment. It was supposed to be a new beginning.

At first, I thought maybe we could build something stable in that apartment. Maybe, just maybe, if I provided enough peace, structure and love, something would click into place.

But I quickly realized, I was the only one building.

There were cracks in the foundation and I wasn't the one who made them. He was emotionally distant, dismissive, always drinking or trying to avoid responsibility and accountability. I poured into him.

My time
My energy
My resources

All to be met with apathy, criticism and control. He didn't want me around, but didn't want me to go either. He liked the idea of me more than the reality of me:

Driven
Successful
Independent
Vocal

He used to say things like, "You just always around," or "You don't know how to give a man space," and my favorite, "You don't know how to be in a relationship." That last comment caused so much confusion for me... my internal dialogue went as follows:

"What type of example do you have? Furthermore, what type of example do you have of even being a man... I'll wait. You have not one healthy example to even compare sooooo..."

No matter how much I tried to respect his space, I was always too much.

When I got the office space, I thought I was helping. In actuality, I was being gaslit, manipulated and controlled. I honestly thought that by changing environments and aiming for a fresh start we would finally be able to progress. I had on rose colored glasses and was in denial of what the reality of the situation was and who he really was. At some point his mask fell off and he could no longer hide who and what he truly was.

A.
Full.
Blown.
Narcissist.

We played house for the next few years and eventually in October of 2022, all hell broke loose and shit hit the fan.

I will never forget the words that uttered from his mouth: "Everybody thinks there's something spectacular about you, but there's nothing spectacular about you to me and you feel that way about yourself."

I was given two options. Let the relationship kill me or save myself. I chose myself.

But right when I thought I was in the clear, he had a health scare of course.

One morning he was complaining about his eye hurting and feeling uncomfortable. He already had procedures done for his glaucoma. He went to the bathroom so he could look at his eye.

"Wendy, come here, look at my eye and see if it looks weird to you."

I looked at his eye and sure enough, it looked like a grey rock had completely covered the retina and pupil area. I immediately called his eye doctor, described what was going on and they wanted to see him as soon as he could get there.

We wasted no time hopping in the car and rushing to their office.

At this point, we both were worried and concerned and put our differences aside. I didn't hate him. He's still a person and I was genuinely concerned about his health and wellbeing.

When we arrived at their office, they escorted us back to an exam room. When the doctor came in, she started asking questions so she could get a better understanding about what was happening.

She asked, "When did you start to feel the discomfort?"

He replied, "This morning when I woke up. My eye was hurting. It felt like I had something in it and my vision was hazy and grey."

She proceeded to examine his left eye. She also examined the right eye as well.

"Well, it looks like a rock has surfaced to the front of your eye," she said. "I have never seen one this big before. We need to get you into surgery immediately. Also, by looking at your right eye, I can see a small rock trying to surface and that will need to be taken care of sooner than later."

An emergency cataract surgery was now on the agenda, so I stayed another week. Not because I had to, but because I still had compassion. Despite everything.

Once the surgery date was scheduled, we followed the detailed instructions given by the doctor. He was given a regimen of medication to take to try to dissolve the rock as much as he could.

We also went over all the aftercare instructions and asked any questions we had in regard to recovery time and follow-up appointments. All of our questions were answered and we were prepared for the Monday morning surgery.

The surgery was successful and quick. He was instructed to rest for the remainder of the day and to use the drops given as instructed. I had to take him to his follow-up appointment the next day so they could reexamine his eye. Everything looked good. Now the healing process could take place.

I took this extra time I had to try selling more of my things and wrapping up more of my business and personal affairs.

I wanted to make sure he was as comfortable as possible before I left and he had what he needed because I knew he wouldn't have much help.

I prepped meals, made sure the kitchen was stocked with easy-to-heat food. I organized his documents and bills. I made sure his coffee was in reach, that the medications were lined up in labeled pill boxes. I cooked rice and peppers, the "jail food" he liked, spaghetti, chicken, soups, snacks, fruit, frozen pizza, everything.

Not because I owed him.
Because I wasn't just trying to leave him helpless and for dead...

He didn't expect me to really leave. He never did. Even then, as I moved silently through the apartment gathering my final items, he thought I was bluffing. But I wasn't.

Thanksgiving came and we went to a family gathering. I thought maybe we could just get through it without drama. But of course, the night ended in chaos. Normally, he'd get drunk and ruin everything. But this time, one of his family members, his cousin, beat him to it.

Prior to the altercation, I pulled her to the side, outside and told her I was leaving in the morning and why. I explained to her in as much detail as I could in the short amount of time I had, that for years I have been abused, disrespected, humiliated and the list goes on and on.

"I cannot continue to live in an environment that will eventually kill me," I said. "He is a narcissist and has been mentally, verbally, emotionally, financially and spiritually abusing me for years and I can't take it anymore."

She was enraged.

Also, by her being semi-drunk didn't help the situation.

We went back in the house and she just kept staring at him with deathly daggers in her eyes. She never gave off that I told her what was going on but he assumed I did. So, in his defense he started saying to her, "what's your problem, why are you looking at me like that." She still didn't say anything. All of a sudden, she started cussing him out, calling him all kinds of "pieces of shit" and everything else he was... she told no lies. That shut down the gathering and we got in our car and went home.

Assuming that I told her what was going on, he used it as an excuse to unleash on me during the hour-long car ride home.

He called me everything but my name. Insulted my character, my dreams, my womanhood. And then added another insult to the mix, "There's nothing special about you." He said with such confidence. So not only was there nothing great and spectacular about me... now there was also nothing special.

When we got back to the apartment, I didn't argue. I didn't scream. I just knew, this was it. The next morning, I was leaving.

I said to him, "And this is why I'm leaving."

The house was dark when we got home. He staggered up the stairs and into the bedroom, still drunk, slurring curses under his breath as if they were prayers. I didn't follow. I didn't say another word.

I thought to myself, "Good, now I can finish packing in peace."

I pulled my car around, quietly loading the final few boxes I had stashed over the last month. I moved with precision, measuring every step, every breath, every motion, like a woman on a mission. I tucked away my documents, my clothes, my hard drives, my vision boards. The bear my parents gave me, Baby Girl, who symbolizes my inner child, was buckled in the front seat and ready to go. I made sure my gun was close by. This wasn't paranoia. It was preparation. I no longer put anything past him.

Sleep was light that night, but I didn't need much. My spirit was already driving south.

By 6:00 a.m., I was in the shower, letting the water wash over me like a baptism. I didn't cry. I didn't tremble. I just breathed. Intentionally. Purposefully. Then I dressed, checked my list, zipped my bags. I took one last look around the apartment. Everything I needed was with me. What I left behind was no longer mine to carry.

He was quieter than usual that morning. His eyes still low from the alcohol, but maybe, just maybe, he felt the weight of finality settling in.

He made me sandwiches for the road. Packed snacks. Gave me $600 in cash, his borrowed share of the rent. I gave him $100 of it back because I knew he didn't have any money and because, despite everything, I still had humanity in me.

He said, "I just wanted to make sure you had something in your pocket while you were driving."

I nodded.
He added, "Stop playing, you're coming back."
"No," I said gently. "No one's playing."

Walking down the stairs to my car, all that kept repeating in my mind was, "you're almost there, you're almost there, just a few more steps."

I made it! I made it to the car. My chest was tight and my heart was beating fast. As I started the engine, tears rolled down my face. Not out of sadness but because of joy, relief and uncertainty.

I didn't tell anyone I was leaving until I was well on the road. I wanted to protect my peace, make sure nothing could stop me, not guilt, not fear, not even concern from the people who loved me. I called my mother and one close friend from the highway, letting them know I was safe and already enroute.

Isolation had been a tool during this process. I knew if I'd let others in too early, their worries or opinions might have clouded the clarity I'd fought to find. I had to make this decision on my own. But my parents had always been there for me, even if our relationship had its own strains, they were still my safety net. They would've driven up and packed my entire life into a U-Haul if I'd only asked.

But this was something I needed to do myself. For myself.

I had to play it cool and strategically. I didn't trust him not to react or retaliate.

Over the years he would constantly say, "If you ever leave me, I'll kill you," I believed him.

He was the type that had to be in control of everything and everyone. As soon as he felt he was losing control and not the center of attention, he would lash out in erratic ways. You couldn't tell me he didn't have multiple personalities on top of being a narcissist.

I remember, I had a photoshoot scheduled early one Saturday morning. He knew I had a photoshoot. I was so excited and had been talking about it for over a month. I was due for a portfolio update with one of the top photographers in Chicago. I got up early to make sure I didn't have to rush and so I could prepare myself both mentally and physically. I had several garment bags full of clothes and a large suitcase filled with shoes, accessories and everything else I would potentially need. I always over pack but I'd rather be overly prepared than not have enough. Fortunately, he was so "kind" to help me bring my luggage and bags down the three flights of stairs to my car.

The photoshoot was amazing. It lasted about three hours and I got exactly what I needed. When I got home, he had the audacity to tell me that he thought I was trying to leave him.

"I thought you were leaving me and never coming back," he said.

"Huh," was my response in pure confusion. "I was at my photoshoot," I replied slowly with a long pause and a look of confusion on my face.

That's when the threat came...

"I thought you were leaving me. You filled your car up with all those clothes and you didn't say too much this morning," he said.

In my mind I was thinking, "what was I supposed to say? It's hard to talk to someone that's drunk and I didn't want any problems."

I just politely said, "No, just went to my photoshoot like I told you."

"Good," he said. "If you did, I would find you and kill you. You don't want to play with me. If you ever try to leave me, I will kill you... And if you are with someone, I'll kill them too."

I just looked at him, rolled my eyes and said, "ok," and walked away so I could get settled and unpack my clothes.

I couldn't believe this man...THEEE AUDACITY.

I actually did try a few times. When things became too overwhelming, I would get a one-way ticket to my parent's house and go visit them for a while.

"When are you coming back," he would ask.

"I don't know," would always be my response.

I think the longest I stayed away was for two weeks. After pleading, begging and making empty promises, I went back hoping it would be different that time around, but in actuality, things would always get worse.

He would say, "If you ever leave me, I will kill you." He made sure he drilled that into my mind and placed fear in my heart.

Honestly, the only time I feared the threat was when I was in his presence. If I left, he would not be able to find me. I recall another time I left for a few days so I could sort some things out and come up with a plan.

He left one morning to go to one of his friend's funeral and I left shortly after him to complete a closing. Since I left after, I was able to pack a bag and leave without any problems. I planned to be gone over the weekend. I was just not going to come home after my closing. I rented a room for the weekend and went no contact. He called, but I didn't answer. A part of me wanted to teach him a lesson and to make him worry...Just like I would worry about him when he wouldn't come home some nights, wouldn't call or answer his phone. I broke down and told someone that I trusted and that we mutually had a connection with. I let them know I was ok and what was going on. I did talk to them a few times while I was there. They were a support for me through this shit show of a relationship.

When I finally did return home, he was in bed, drunk I assume. The energy in the house was thick and very dark. I just came in and went straight to my room. He got up but didn't say much. The next day he acted like nothing ever happened... BUT he made sure to tell me that I need to be careful.

"If you try to leave me, I will kill you," were the words that mumbled from his mouth.

We did have guns in the house and one of my biggest fears was that he would try to scare me in the night by pulling it out on me in my sleep and waking me up with a gun in my face or pulling it out on me in a moment of anger and rage

My Breaking Point

I have reached my breaking point. I cannot heal in the same environment that broke me and you cannot heal me... you were the one I allowed to break me.

I see now how I allowed you to disrespect me, devalue me and treat me like everything except an equal partner. I allowed the manipulation, the gaslighting, the financial, emotional, verbal and even physical abuse. I hate to admit it, but it happened. And while you may never acknowledge the harm, I cannot pretend it didn't exist.

I was conditioned to beg for help, to carry the entire weight of "us" on my back, to exhaust myself while you sat entitled and unbothered. I altered my values, my spirit and even my body just to avoid conflict and keep some version of peace that never really existed.

You told me lies about who I was until I began to believe them:

I was worthless, unlovable, hard to deal with, not good enough. You projected your wounds onto me and convinced me they were mine. And for years, I carried that weight.

But here's the truth: I gave you my heart, my soul, my loyalty and my effort. And it still wasn't enough, because the problem was never me.

What broke me wasn't just your words, actions or betrayals, it was the moment I started to believe them. It was the moment I asked myself, "Why am I even here?"

But this is also my why. This is why I'm choosing differently now. Why I refuse to keep spiraling. Why I'm reclaiming my worth, my peace and my power.

You may never take accountability or heal your own trauma. That's not my responsibility anymore. The only person I can control, protect and heal is myself. And that's exactly what I'm doing, starting now.

Chapter 3

Freedom

"A survivor is someone who endured loss or harm, adapted to what could not be undone and continued forward. Survival is not victory; it is persistence under altered conditions. Freedom comes not from what was overcome, but from no longer being controlled by what happened."

I'm free.

I'm finally, truly, undeniably free. And I felt it in my bones before I even hit the highway.

This wasn't just any eight-hour drive. This was the physical manifestation of emotional release, a detox in motion. A journey of shedding. Shedding pain, shedding lies, shedding years of disappointment and exhaustion I had carried like bricks in a bag no one else could see.

The sun was shining and it felt like a spotlight on my rebirth. The wind danced differently that day. My heart pounded with a mixture of fear and joy. I was terrified as I drove into my new life. My new beginning. The tears came early, even before I hit the interstate, tears of relief, gratitude, frustration, anger, sadness and the list goes on. I didn't try to stop them. It was purging. It was healing. I could finally breathe, exhale all the built-up pain and distress.

My brown Cadillac SRX was packed to capacity. You would've thought I was leaving the country with the way every inch of that car was stacked. I couldn't see out the rear-view mirror or back window at all and my side views were narrowed with only access to the side-view mirrors. But my path ahead? Clear. Crystal clear.

Baby Girl sat beside me, strapped into the front seat like a passenger on a freedom ride. She wasn't just a stuffed toy. She represented everything I had fought to protect:

My softness.
My inner child.

My innocence.

She was not only my inner child, she was my silent cheerleader and emotional support. I clutched her when I cried. I clutched her when I slept. I looked to her for that emotional, one-way sounding board. I was also there to protect her, reparent her, love her and in return, I was protecting myself, reparenting myself and loving myself.

My gun sat within reach, tucked just right. That's how serious I had to be about protecting my peace. That's how real the fear still was. You don't leave someone like him without considering every possibility.

Once I made the official decision to leave, I had to make sure I did so in a safe, unconfrontational, non-hostile way. I played everything calm, cool and collected. I avoided the arguments, blocked out the gaslighting, ignored the mental, emotional and verbal abuse. This time was truly a test. My PTSD and C-PTSD were consistently triggered. I pulled out every tool I had in my toolbox to survive those horrible 3 weeks before leaving. I increased my therapy sessions to twice a week, made sure I was praying, meditating, journaling and making sure I was taking care of my physical wellbeing. I also intentionally found things to do outside of the house for relaxation, peace of mind and for escape. At this point I didn't care what he did. If he wanted to drink his life away, so be it. If he wanted to continue to confirm every reason I had for leaving, go right ahead. Make my job easier. There is a song by Dru Hill that I still listen to today called, "One Good Reason." The song basically asks to be given "ONE" good reason why to stay. I couldn't think of one. PERIOD! At one point during the course of the relationship, I attended Al-anon meetings. They were a support group for family, friends and loved ones of alcoholics. The meetings, support and literature were very helpful. I gained a better understanding of what I was dealing with and how to detach. It came to the point where I had to take an honest look at my situation. Not what I hoped, wished and prayed it was or could be, but what it actually was in the present day and time. I was looking at it with the same potential I was looking at him with. The harsh reality I was faced with asking myself was, "What kind of life was I living if I had to detach?" I wanted to experience a present love. A healthy love. A love that is kind, patient and reciprocal. Then there was another layer to my reality and additional questions I had to ask myself. "What and where are the parts of myself that I am not loving? The parts that I am abusing? The Parts that I am neglecting and not showing up for? The parts that I am ignoring and detaching from?" When I honestly sat down and answered those questions, shame, sadness, embarrassment and anger took over. I had lost myself in him. In the relationship. I realized that the most important relationship I should have developed FRIST, was the one with myself and anything outside of that was a bonus. I was looking for outside love and validation, when all along I should have had that within myself. Self-love, self assurance and validation. I also recall attending several CoDA meetings. Codependents Anonymous was a 12-step program to help individuals develop healthy and functional relationships. One book that helped me heal my codependency was "Codependent No More" by Melody Beattie. I was introduced to that book when I first went to therapy after he left me for his child's mother the first time. I had no idea what codependency was. This made me look at every relationship in my life, not just the one with him.

Healing has many forms. Therapy, prayer, meditation, journaling. For me, one of the most sacred tools was music. As I drove, my playlist was on repeat with 5 significant songs. They weren't just background noise. They were my soul's lifeline.

Over and over.
Repeat.
Volume on max.
Each lyric, a stitch in the wounds that needed closing.

"Cuff It" by Beyoncé was my reckless joy. In the middle of my pain, this song reminded me what it felt like to be carefree again, to move my body, to laugh, to remember there was still fun left in me. It was medicine disguised as a dance beat. "Energy" by Beyoncé was my shift. Away from him. Away from the karmic pull. Into myself. Into sovereignty. Every time it played, I could feel my spirit reclaiming its power, like my soul was rearranging itself into alignment. "Break My Soul" by Beyoncé was my anthem. My declaration to the universe. Every lyric was me standing taller, saying, *"You tried to break me, but I'm still here."* It was survival in song form, a rallying cry that carried me through the nights when I wasn't sure I could make it. "Flowers" by Miley Cyrus This song reminded me of my worth. That I could love myself better than anyone who tried to tear me down. It was a promise to myself. I don't have to wait for someone else to validate me. I can buy myself flowers, dance alone and feel whole. "Superwoman" by Karyn White—this one cut the deepest. I played it when the tears threatened to steal my voice. When I felt invisible and exhausted from carrying everything on my shoulders. It gave me permission to admit I was hurting, that I wasn't invincible and that was okay.

Receiving calls from my parents, a few friends and family members, checking in with me to make sure I was safe and in the best spirits I could be in despite the circumstances, made me know I was loved and supported, which was comforting and confirmation that I would not be alone in this new journey.   And yes, *he* called too, still in shock that I was actually gone. Probably assuming I'd answer with regret or fear and make the decision to turn around and go back.

"Why are you doing this to me", were the words that had the audacity to pass through his lips.

There were so many things I could have said but I didn't have the mental energy to entertain the bait.

I countered his question with a question.

"Why did you do this to me?"

He was speechless and wanted to hurry up and get off the phone.

"Fine by me", I thought. "Let me drive in peace."

I did appreciate him calling to check on me but each time caused anxiety and disturbed my spirit.

"Don't act like you care now. You had your chance. And again, I could not think of ONE GOOD REASON," were the thoughts that ran through my mind.

He would want to have the same conversation over and over again.

"I'm not having this conversation with you. If this is what you are calling to talk about, DO. NOT. CALL. ME", I finally had to tell him.

What's crazy is... we had been best friends once. That's the part people don't get. There *were* good moments. We shared laughter, inside jokes, music, late-night drives. We were both foodies so we'd hit up every restaurant we could find, always toasting something. Our bond with music ran deep. We'd sit in the car for hours, sipping cocktails, sharing lyrics, dissecting beats like it was our love language. And at that time it was.

But none of that changes the damage. None of that outweighed the pain.

I had to choose myself.

Even in the quiet moments on that highway, when I thought of the smiles, the playlists, the "remember whens," I never once regretted leaving.

Because even though I had love for him, even though a piece of me would always care about his well-being, I finally saw it for what it was. He had disrespected me too many times. Dismissed me. Belittled me. He had shown me who he was.

And the truth is? I had seen straight through him. To his core. I knew his pain. I knew his trauma. I even knew his potential. But all of that didn't change the fact that he was emotionally destructive.

Potential means nothing if the person refuses to grow. And I couldn't carry his brokenness on my back anymore.

Free At Last

*"I will no longer shrink myself to fit
into places that break me.
I will no longer allow disrespect,
manipulation or abuse in any form.
I will no longer carry burdens that are not mine to bear.
I will no longer believe the lies spoken over me.*

*I choose to honor my worth.
I choose to reclaim my voice.
I choose to stand in my truth.*

*I choose to love myself deeply and unapologetically.
What once broke me has now awakened me.
I am free. I am healing. I am whole."*

Chapter 4

Welcome Home

"Settled is when the body no longer feels in danger and the nervous system relaxes out of survival mode. It is the state where tension eases, breathing slows and you are able to think clearly, feel present and respond instead of react."

Pulling into my parents' driveway, was like the earth exhaled with me.

They were standing outside, already waiting. My mother was standing on the side of the driveway, hands clasped and waiting for me to pull all the way in. My father was near the garage door, trying to act casual but pacing like he wanted to run to me. Even "our" puppy, Munchkin, was anticipating my arrival. I opened the car door and before I could even step out fully, my mother had her arms around me. We didn't say anything at first.

We just cried.

It wasn't a sob. It was that deep, low cry, the kind that comes from the gut. The kind that only makes sense when you've finally escaped something you never thought you'd get out of.

We held each other for what felt like an hour but was probably just a minute. My father placed his hand gently on my back and said, "You're home now." And at that moment, I was.

They helped me unload the car, what we couldn't fit in the house, we placed on the covered porch. Bag by bag, box by box, piece by piece... I was unpacking not just belongings, but fragments of my former life. Each one heavy with memory.

I moved into their spare room. They made it comforting and inviting.

That first night, I barely slept. My body was home, but my nervous system was still back there, on edge, waiting for the next outburst, the next insult, the next unpredictable shift in energy.

I laid in that bed and stared at the ceiling. Then at the fan. Then at the shadowy corners of the room. I cried, again. Not loud this time. Just silent tears running sideways into the pillow. I went into a daze.

I thought about all the times I would lay in my bed, waiting to hear for proof of life and movement in the apartment in the mornings. That was when I knew it was safe to start the day. It was ok to start making noise. Making breakfast, opening the blinds and giving our home life. Since we had our own rooms, I made my room into my sanctuary... my office. It was my get away. When he got tired of me or I snored too loud, I would sleep in my room and he in his. On several occasions I experimented. If I snored through the night, he would wake me up. Push, shove, hit, kick me, to wake me up. I started to just lay there sometimes, just to see if he was torturing me intentionally and sure enough he was. There were instances where I was not sleeping and therefore not snoring, but yet and still he would push, shove, kick and hit me to "wake me up." He was just downright evil. Once he got up and started moving around, it was ok to get up and start the day.

I recall waking up on my 40th birthday. I felt good. I felt like a brand-new woman. I was happy, healthy and alive. I was in my room dancing and singing and enjoying myself. All of a sudden he burst into my room and cussed me out.

"What the fuck are you doing? Why are you making so much noise? I am trying to sleep. You are so stupid. You just don't know how to be a woman and respect a man," were the words he screamed at me. It was my birthday. All the calls and texts were coming in full force and he hated that. I was on face time with his aunt and all she could do was drop her jaw in disbelief at what she just saw me experience. She was in tears with me experiencing this moment. On this day which was supposed to be special. He knew how to ruin any and everything. I gathered myself and started to feel better. I refused to let him ruin my special day.

This was a painful and heart wrenching memory and reflection. But it was my truth. A truth I lived through and survived. I realized I was free. I was safe and it was time to reclaim Wendy.

The timing of it all was divine. My parents were preparing for a trip to Aruba and would be gone for three weeks. That meant I would have the house to myself, just me and my little Munchkin.

They made sure I was set before they left. Groceries. Instructions. Comfort. Hugs. Reassurance.

My mother made sure she comforted me. Reassuring me that everything would be alright and to take this time to relax, heal and take care of myself. She told me not to worry about the details of the living arrangements and we would sort all of that out when they got back. There was no pressure, no stress, just the opportunity to gain clarity and sit with myself and with my feelings.

They left two days later. And I was alone. Not lonely. Alone. And I needed that. I needed the quiet. The space. The freedom to do *nothing*.

Rock bottom

There are moments in life where it feels like everything is collapsing. Career, relationships, finances, health. For me, one of those moments came when I was forced to choose between losing myself completely or finding a way to heal. What I didn't know at the time was that rock bottom would push me into a new path of spiritual awakening and healing that would change my life forever.

Chapter 5

The Rebirth

*"Healing is the deliberate process
of restoring agency, stability and self-trust after harm.
It requires acknowledging reality without denial,
integrating experience and establishing boundaries and
patterns that support safety and growth. Healing does not
erase the past; it transforms its impact and reclaims control
over one's life."*

Those first weeks, I could barely move. I had no strength to clean, no motivation to get dressed, no desire to be productive. I stayed mostly in bed. Sinking into the mattress as if it was a big cloud. My mom started calling my bed, "the trauma bed." And she wasn't wrong.

That bed became my nest, my bunker, my cocoon. A place to cry, sleep, zone out, binge YouTube and other social media, write in my journal or simply stare into space.

I kept the door cracked just enough for Munchkin to come and go as he pleased. He's a coco-colored miniature Pincher, with big, bright, brown eyes. He wouldn't leave for long anyway. He always came back. He knew I needed him. I needed his love and comforting presence. I love how animals can sense when you need them, can sense good energy and the kindness, safety and innocence in people. They can also sense illnesses in people. I was all the above. Developed chronic illnesses yet kind, safe and with an innocent spirit. He was my little protector. He was my caregiver just like I was his.

The silence in the house felt sacred. It was just what I needed. No yelling. No slamming doors. No walking on eggshells. Just the hum of the refrigerator, the occasional bark from Munchkin and the sound of my own breath, uneven, but mine.

At first, I didn't know what to do with all that space. All that time. All that *freedom*.

I told myself, "This year is for healing."

No dating.
No entertaining old patterns.
No numbing with busyness.
Just healing.

A complete rebirth.

It sounded noble. But in practice, it was brutal.

Thanks to the insurance settlement from my office burning down, which actually turned out to be a blessing, I was able to take the necessary time for myself, my healing and to figure out how I wanted my life to look like moving forward. I was starting with a clean slate. It was broken, but it was my broken clean slate and I could put it back together anyway I wanted. I could be whoever I wanted. It was exciting and I was looking forward to healing into the new me and my new life.

I journaled every day—sometimes writing until my hand cramped. I wrote out memories, triggers, dreams, nightmares, prayers and confessions. I felt this would help my healing process. To have everything, every incident, every word, I could remember, right smack in my face. I couldn't run and hide anymore and just brush it under the rug and pretend like everything was fine. That I was fine. I was not. I had to face everything head on in order to start the brutal and painful healing process. I had to look in the mirror and face the honest and raw truths about myself, my situation and begin to process WHY. I stripped myself down to my core and started evaluating my values, my boundaries, my connections and interactions. Also, what and who was in my life that was not healthy and not for my greater good and in alignment with where I was going in my life and the new chapter I was writing. I had to question my beliefs and recall the experiences from my childhood. I had to get to the nitty gritty. I had a journal for shadow work. I had a journal for inner-child healing. I had a positivity and gratitude journal. I had all the tools I needed. I was determined to push through and become the best WHOLE version of myself. I was not in a rush. I was able to take my time. When I would become stuck, I would reach out and get professional help and guidance. I am an advocate for therapy. Therapy and medication has helped me get through some of my darkest moments. Journaling has also helped me get through my darkest moments. This book actually started off as a series of journal entries and poems. Some pages were soaked with tears. Others were filled with curses in all caps. And were!

Journal Entry:

December 1, 2022:

How did I get here? What did I do to deserve this? I'm not a bad person. I'm so angry with myself. How could I have allowed this man to treat me like he did? Was I that unhappy within myself? Did I not love myself enough to know my value and my worth? I am the victim but I will not take on a victim mindset. I did play a part in all of this and I will hold myself accountable. Yes, I did allow the treatment, the words, the disrespect. Yes, I could have walked away at any time. Even though I can admit that I allowed this, that doesn't excuse the shitty behavior and treatment. Just because you can do something and someone allows it, doesn't mean you should. He had a choice about how he treated me and he chose to use and abuse me. I can't believe I lost myself and forgot who I was. I don't even recognize myself anymore. Who am I? I hate the person I became while with him. I hated my life with him. I was dying inside. Every day I felt like I was fighting for my life. I had to protect myself mentally and emotionally. I am free now but I am so lost. I have no idea what is next. I walked away from everything. Everything I worked hard for. My possessions, my businesses, my career... everything. Now I have to figure out what is next. I know I have a long way to go but I'm just going to take it one day at a time and be kind and patient with myself. It is now my responsibility to heal. To dig deep and understand why. Why did I allow this? Why did I feel like I had no choice and had to settle? I know I was in a bad place mentally and emotionally when I came back from LA. I was vibrating on a very low frequency and now knowing what I know, you attract what is on that same frequency. People, environments, situations etc. But

DAMN!!!! I'm not a shitty person. So now I am on a healing journey to fill in the gaps and put the broken pieces of my puzzle back together better than ever. I am ready for the challenge!

I'm praying. Not always formally. Sometimes I just want to lay here and whisper to the Divine and Universe, "Please. Please give me the strength, knowledge, wisdom, protection, discernment and healing to navigate through this time. I know that there is a reason I had to go through this experience and I know it was for my highest and greater good. Just please help and guide me through it."

Other times I just feel like lighting incense and candles and chanting until my voice goes hoarse. I'm pulling all kinds of cards. Tarot cards, Oracle cards, affirmation cards, empowering questions cards, whatever felt right that day. At this point I'm willing to try anything to fight for my healing. My healing is personal. I cannot allow myself to sit in this pain. The funny thing is this pain I'm feeling is actually fueling me and giving me hope and motivation. I know I could make it to the other side whole and happy.

Listening to and watching RC Blakes and Dr. Romani on YouTube is giving me life and hope. Their voices fill the empty spaces in my heart. Their messages and teachings help me stay grounded when my mind starts spinning. They are helping to bring me back to life. They are giving me a better understanding of what I had been through, am currently going through and how the other side can look and feel. They are helping me restore my confidence and to recognize and know my worth. Of course, they are not the end all be all but it sure is a start in the right direction. I am determined to heal on purpose every day.

Chapter 6

The Body Keeps Score

"Trauma-informed healing is an approach that recognizes the impact of trauma on the nervous system, behavior and identity and integrates this awareness into recovery. It prioritizes safety, autonomy and agency. It treats survival responses as adaptations rather than pathology and avoids re-traumatization by restoring regulation, choice and self-trust through intentional, respectful and paced intervention."

It was time to bring in additional reinforcements. There was only so much I could do on my own. I had more questions that needed answers and there were blockages I couldn't work through on my own. I started going to therapy again. Weekly sessions with a trauma-informed therapist and an accountability coach through a telehealth program.

My therapist helped me process things I never said out loud.

My coach helped me set small initial goals like getting out of bed, drinking more water, getting out of the house to get some fresh air and eating real food.

The next 6 weeks were intense. One talked me through the pain, the flashbacks, the feelings of unworthiness. The other held me accountable. Gently helping me build routines and regain structure.

While I was healing mentally, emotionally and spiritually, I began to realize how sick and unhealthy I was. Once your body knows you are safe and no longer in a state of distress, it relaxes and everything you've been suppressing surfaces. I realized the severity of my declined health and how much I neglected myself and treated myself so poorly.

A visit to the doctor confirmed what I already knew... my health was in shambles.

I was almost 200 pounds. My blood pressure was dangerously high. My A1C was through the roof—diabetic levels. I had chronic fatigue and insomnia. My cholesterol was sky high. My body had been holding every ounce of stress, fear and shame. It was literally shutting down. I knew I had to change my lifestyle and get intentional.

My insurance covered a gym membership, so I joined.
I got a personal trainer as a birthday gift to myself.
I swam three to four times a week.
Used the sauna.
Sat in the hot tub and let the heat melt some of the tension out of my bones.

On days I didn't make it to the gym, I swam in my parents' pool. Sometimes my mom would join and we'd float or do water aerobics to music—just laughing, just moving, just *living*.

One thing I learned and whole heartedly believe is that the body keeps score. It holds on to everything unhealed and what you are unable to release and let go.

When I stopped ignoring my pain,
I started hearing my truth.

I used to rush self-care like it was a chore. I'd sit through nail appointments impatiently, feeling guilty for taking time for myself. Somewhere deep inside, I didn't believe I deserved peace or softness.

The only space I truly allowed myself to breathe was during my massages and facials. Three quiet hours once a month where the world faded and I could simply exist. That was my sanctuary, my way of saying, *"I'm still here."*

It was during one of those sessions that my therapist noticed a lump on my back. Doctors said it was my spine shifting and pushing against some tissue, but I knew better. I pushed for answers and discovered several lipomas, large and heavy, pressing against my shoulder blades. They weren't dangerous, but they told a story. The story of me carrying everyone's weight but my own.

In addition to the lipomas, I had a recurring boil on my ass that wouldn't go away that needed to be addressed and taken care of as well. The surgeon said we would address both issues... since he was going to be back there anyway. I loved how he brought humor to the situation.

The surgeries went well, but the healing was harder. I was alone, in pain, still surrounded by someone who didn't know how to show up for me. When I asked for help one night, I was yelled at, left crying in the dark still trying to comfort myself through the hurt.

I had no other choice than to do what I've always done. Show up for myself.

After the medicine wore off and some of the swelling went away, it was time to check in with the doctor so he could clean my wounds, drain the fluid from my back, redress and pack me. I ended up having to drive myself an hour each way to every follow-up appointment, twice a week, even when I wasn't supposed to sit or drive. My body was weak, but my spirit was determined.

Later, when the boil returned, when anger once again rose to the surface, I finally understood what my body had been trying to tell me. The boils were my buried rage. The lipomas were my burdens. My body had been carrying my unspoken pain.

Healing has taught me to listen.
When my shoulders ache, I ask what I'm holding.
When my chest feels heavy, I pause and breathe. My body no longer has to scream to be heard.
I'm listening now.

The Body Remembers

The body remembers what the mind learned to bury.
It keeps the echoes, the tension, the pauses—not to hurt you,
but because it wasn't safe to let go before.

Your shoulders, your breath, your heartbeat—
they tell stories you never spoke.

This isn't weakness.
It's evidence of survival.

Healing isn't erasing the past—
it's gently returning to it
with compassion, patience and presence.

As you breathe, soften and listen,
the body finally learns—

It doesn't have to hold everything alone anymore.

Chapter 7

The Shift

"Boundaries are defined limits that protect an individual's autonomy, time and well-being within relationships, family systems, environments and one's own internal behavior. They determine what is acceptable, what is not and what will no longer be tolerated, functioning to prevent harm, preserve agency and maintain psychological and emotional safety."

Making excellent progress physically and mentally, there was still a lot of underlining, unaddressed family trauma.

Being around my parents after so many years away was... complicated.

We hadn't lived under the same roof in over 20 years. Our rhythms didn't match. Our communication styles clashed. We didn't know each other intimately at this stage in our lives and it was an adjustment for all of us.. I was grateful for having a safe place to come to. A place I called home.

My mom in particular, had this anxious, often condescending energy that rubbed against my raw, sensitive state. Our relationship was strained. We know each other but at the same time we don't. One day, she said she read something about apologizing to someone you've hurt. So she turned to me and said, "I guess I should apologize to you", sarcastically.

I said, "You should."

She offered a half-hearted, vague apology. I told her, "You've always hurt me."

And that was that.

She brushed it off with a defense mechanism she's used for years. But I had changed. I wasn't a little girl anymore. I wasn't going to stay silent to protect other people's comfort. I had found my voice.

And I was going to use it.

I also had to establish healthy boundaries. That was a big thing for me. Establishing boundaries where there were none.

I told my parents plainly, "I need space. I need respect. I'm healing. Please don't ask me a million questions. Don't force me into things I'm not ready for. Let me go through this in my way." I requested this because yes, I wanted to be able to heal the way I needed to and that was best for me, but also, so I wouldn't project anything on them that they didn't deserve or had nothing to do with.

They tried. But old habits die hard. I had to keep reminding them of this boundary I was setting and enforcing.

I was a person who didn't have boundaries with anyone. Well, not healthy and firm ones anyway. I walked around with rose colored glasses when it came to certain people and situations. They could do no wrong, wouldn't dare hurt me...until they did. I had to start evaluating the connections in my life and see where boundaries needed to be set. I needed to determine the access levels that I would allow moving forward. I wrote down everyone I could think of that I knew and placed them in separate categories based on our relationship and interaction. I looked at each name and evaluated the energy and thoughts I got by just looking at their name. How did it make me feel? How have my interactions been with this person? Where do they fit in my life at this present moment? I had a lot of honest work to do. It was an emotional process but I pushed through and felt a heavy weight lifted from my shoulders.

I did however have to keep my parents and Brian in separate categories. Those relationships needed a different kind of evaluation and attention.

Even though I left and was on my healing journey, I still remained in communication with him. For some reason despite everything, the trauma bond still hadn't been completely severed and if I'm being completely honest, for some twisted reason, talking to him soothed me in some way. Just knowing he was hurting, confused, didn't understand and knowing he messed up, gave me some form of relief and satisfaction. I never wished harm on him or had any ill will. His karma was me leaving. You can't outrun karma and I had the opportunity to see it up close and personally turn him every which way but loose.

The conversations we continued to have were triggers in disguise.
They started off friendly.
They ended in arguments.

He'd call, trying to be charming.
But soon the jabs would come. The guilt trips. The gaslighting.

He'd say, "You always planned to leave."
Or, "You just ran home to mommy and daddy."

AND DID!

Sometimes I hung up mid-sentence.
Other times I argued back, even though I knew better.

It was like trying to reason with a hurricane.

And then, there were the flashbacks.
I remembered being tortured and tormented.

I remember being told I was a piece of shit.

A nothing ass bitch.

And the famous nail it the coffin. "There is nothing spectacular about you to me."

Those memories came like waves. Some small. Some tidal. But every time I processed one, I reclaimed a piece of myself.

Eventually, I stopped being so available.
Eventually, I stopped waking up in a panic.
Eventually, I started dreaming again.

I began thinking about what my next chapter would look like. I started dressing up again. Feeling beautiful. I didn't wear makeup—just my lip gloss and moisturizer—but I looked in the mirror and smiled. I liked what I saw.

I reconnected with old friends slowly. Let a few know I was back. But I wasn't ready for company. Just knowing they were there was enough.

I kept journaling.
Kept praying.
Kept pulling cards.
Kept walking the puppy.
Kept swimming.
Kept reclaiming my life.

This was no longer just recovery.
This was resurrection.

I wasn't just surviving anymore.
I was rebuilding.

And piece by piece, I was becoming *me* again.

Allow Me to Reintroduce Myself

You think you know me,
but you only remember the version I outgrew.
The one who kept quiet to keep the peace,
who mistook survival for strength.

I've shed those layers.
I've met the woman underneath the wounds,
and she no longer flinches when someone says "no."
She doesn't shrink to make others comfortable.
She doesn't apologize for her healing.

My silence has turned into boundaries,
my pain into purpose.
I don't move from fear anymore, I move from faith.
Every tear that fell watered who I've become.

So no, you don't know me.
Not this voice. Not this power. Not this peace.
Allow me to reintroduce myself.
I am the woman I was always meant to be.

Chapter 8

Stuck

"A trauma bond is an emotional attachment that can form in an abusive relationship, characterized by the connection the victim feels toward the perpetrator. This bond often develops through cycles of abuse and reconciliation, leading the victim to develop sympathy or affection for the abuser. It is considered an unhealthy attachment that can make it difficult for individuals to leave abusive situations."

The sad truth about a trauma bond is that it can take longer to break than you would like. Even though I was well on my way to becoming whole again, this was one that I couldn't completely shake. A part of me wanted to believe that maybe, just maybe, if he got help, if I stayed the course, if we both committed to our healing, we could reconnect. I knew it was foolish. But trauma bonds don't dissolve with logic. They dissolve with time, distance and brutal honesty. And I wasn't quite there yet.

Meanwhile, my life was transforming and shifting, while his was spiraling. He started drinking more and calling at odd hours. Saying things that made my stomach twist. Still, I responded. I listened. I tried to reason with him. And when things got bad enough, I used every ounce of strength I had left to convince him to go to the emergency room so he could go through a medically supervised detox.

We've gone down that road several times. I remember the first time I was so scared. I heard him in the bathroom falling and ending up on the floor, having a seizure. Our bathroom had two doors. One door led to the hallway and the other was connected to my room. I was in my room and I heard a loud thud and then mumbling noises as if someone was trying to call for help but couldn't get the words or sounds out. I tried to open the door from inside my bedroom, but I couldn't. His body was blocking the door. I ran to the door in the hallway and was able to open it and get to him. I fell to the floor immediately and tried to comfort him while he was still shaking. I started praying and repeating out loud, "Please don't do this. Please don't do this. You can't leave me like this". I had my phone with me and I called 911. I explained to them that he was having a seizure and to please come quick and help me. I was crying and hysterical. I had to remind myself to calm down so that I could think clearly and be there for him. I didn't want him to panic. He was confused and delirious at this point. I never experienced anything like this before. I thought he was dying. When he calmed down, I helped him up and we walked carefully to the living room. I made sure he was comfortable on his section of the couch while we waited for the ambulance to arrive.

Once they arrived, they started checking his vitals, asking him questions to make sure he knew who he was, where he was and if he knew what had just happened. He knew his name, where he was, but couldn't give them the address and he had no idea why they were there and what had just happened. After checking on him, they wanted to get more information from me. They wanted to know how much he had to drink, how often he drinks, how much he drinks normally and has this happened before. It had been a while that day since he had his last drink. He was actually trying to get sober on his own and taper off the alcohol and as a result of the detox symptoms, he had a seizure. He usually could go through 3 pints of Patrone in a day...sometimes more. They gave him the option to go to the hospital to get checked out and go through their detox program. He agreed. They took him while I stayed behind and packed some clothes, toiletries and his charger. He called me when they made it to the hospital. I wasn't too far behind them. When I made it to the hospital, he was already checked in waiting to be seen. I asked for his status and they took me to the area they were keeping him. The emergency room was packed but since he came in the ambulance, they had beds in the hallway in the area where they saw the patients. They wanted to keep an eye on him while he was waiting to be seen. They wanted to make sure he didn't have another episode since he was actively detoxing. They gave us a bucket in case he had to throw up and a urinal in case he had to pee. Even though he still wasn't fully admitted, they still checked on him and gave him some medication to help ease the symptoms and calm him down. It took over 11 hours to finally get completely admitted and a room. He couldn't just be on a regular floor in a regular room, he had to go to the Intensive Care Unit. They had to monitor him closely. They were making sure he didn't have anymore seizures and he was a fall risk so they had the bed set up with the bars up and an alarm if he tried to get up on his own. I made sure the doctors updated me with his progress and vitals. I barely left his side in the hospital. Witnessing his detox process was heartbreaking and traumatizing. To see him like that. So vulnerable, helpless and confused. There were moments where he was hallucinating, talking to people that weren't there, talking in circles. I was so worried, but he was exactly where he needed to be. It even got to the point they had to restrain his arms and legs so he would stop trying to pull the IV out of his arms and stop trying to get up. He was agitated and confused for a few days but he knew I was there and that helped. When he would wake up from resting periods, he would see a friendly, familiar face. The staff knew he had someone who cared for him and he wasn't just someone off the street. He was well kept, clean and particular. After a few days, he was able to calm down and we bribed him with extra food so we could take the restraints off if he would stop trying to pull the IV out and stop trying to get up. I made sure he knew he was loved and had my support. I would even wash him up cause he didn't want them to and I didn't mind. I wanted him to be as comfortable as possible. He stayed in the hospital for about a week and at that time he was not ready to go to rehab. He felt he could get sober on his own. AND we were supposed to be picking up the Slingshot in a few days. They were finally done building it. We had to special order it and it took about a month and a half for them to build it. There was NOOOOO way he was going to miss picking it up and enjoying it. He stopped drinking for about a week and went right back to the old habits. Apparently, he was not scared enough and that was not his rock bottom. And of course, there was not anything I could say to encourage him to keep going.

Convincing him wasn't easy. I had to navigate his pride, his defensiveness and his fear. But eventually, he agreed. I am an advocate for anyone that is willing to help themselves. I'll meet you halfway. Once he agreed to go to detox and rehab, everything moved so quickly. I helped coordinate with his care team, arranging his admittance into a treatment facility. He would start inpatient rehab, followed by sober living. I told myself, "This is my final act of love." I needed to know I had done everything I could before walking away for good.

With him agreeing to go to detox, rehab and sober living, I decided to go back to Chicago to wrap things up at the apartment. The timing felt right. He would be safe, monitored and out of the way. I could move freely. I packed quickly, throwing essentials into the back of my car and began the long, eight-hour drive. Meanwhile, he drove himself to the emergency room, was able to get admitted and start the process. At this point his car was still on the repo list so he was risking them taking it while he was there. Part of the plan was for me to pick up the car and put it in the garage so he wouldn't have to worry about it while he was taking care of himself. I arrived the morning he was scheduled to go to the rehab facility. Unfortunately, I got there too late and they came and got his car between twelve and two in the morning. I was able to see him off and bring a few essentials and clothes to the hospital. I was able to get all the information needed about his car. They were going to hold it for thirty days with the option to extend based on if he was going to redeem it. So he had thirty days to decide whether he wanted to keep his car or not. In the meantime, his focus was getting better.

Now that he was on his way, It was time to go to the apartment, get settled and get some rest. I'd figure everything out later. I knew I would have my work cut out for me. There would be grocery shopping to do, boxes and packing supplies to get, arrangements to be made and business to take care of. Opening the door, I noticed the air was heavy with silence. Everything looked exactly as I'd left it, but somehow colder. Emptier. I stood in the living room for a moment, absorbing the stillness. This had once been our home. Our late-night music sessions. Our laughter. Our arguments. Our silence.

Once I was rested, unpacked and settled, I took inventory of what all I would need so that I could fully be comfortable. I made sure I got my necessities and took a few days to reflect on what was ahead of me for the next several months. I was going to be there for at least a month, if not longer. It was good timing honestly. I got the opportunity to be alone, sit with myself and continue my healing in a different but familiar environment. It also gave my parents a break. LOL.

It felt good to be back in my old home. It was comfortable, familiar and safe. Even though it held so many memories and emotions, this was part of my healing and part of the closure I didn't know I needed.

Walking through the apartment, I realized I left behind so much stuff. I literally packed what I could in my truck and left. I had made peace with it. It was only stuff and stuff could be replaced. I did leave with the most important thing though. I left with my peace and that was worth more than any bedframe or bookshelf.

Since I was going to be there for a while, I decided to try to sell the remaining furniture and items that I had left behind. There was a complete bedroom set. Bed, bedframe with shelves, nightstands, a floor mirror, bookshelf. There was a complete dining set, sectional living room set with an ottoman. It was a lot but I now had the time.

In addition to trying to sell off my remaining items, there was still a lot of business I had to take care of and wrap up. The rent was about 4 months behind and the utilities were about 2 months behind. I was keeping up with the utilities since they were still in my name but It got to the point that I just didn't care anymore and told him he would have to figure it out because I was taking them out of my name.

During COVID we were able to take advantage of the resources they were offering. Rental assistance, utility assistance, unemployment, etc. I randomly received an email saying that it was time to reapply for rental assistance. They were going to pay the back rent and three future months as well as any outstanding utility bills. This was perfect and came right on time. After they took care of that, everything would be caught up and it would be enough time for me to finish wrapping things up, turn over the apartment and leave. I applied, we were approved, they made the payments, it was a done deal. Two important things taken care of.

Knowing he was settled into rehab, I felt a strange relief. For the first time in a long while, I wasn't responsible for managing his moods or monitoring his drinking. I had time to breathe, to process, to prepare for the next step. When he was able to start making phone calls, he would call for brief moments and we would update each other on what was going on. His focus was healing and getting better, while I was wrapping things up and taking care of things on the outside to help make his transition smooth when he completed the program and prepared for sober living. He was making progress and taking it one day at a time. He was feeling good about himself and was looking forward to continuing his healing and recovery process... Until he wasn't.

Meanwhile, I decided that since I was going to be in town for a while, I would take on some notary clients and contact my talent agents so I could do some modeling and acting work. It kept me distracted and I was doing what I enjoyed and loved.

In the beginning he sounded focused, almost hopeful. I let myself believe. Maybe this was the start of his transformation. Maybe all the pain had finally pushed him toward change.

But the illusion didn't last.

Three weeks in, he started mocking the other men in treatment. Making jokes about their efforts to secure halfway house placements. Laughing at their attempts to stay sober. The cynicism was a red flag I couldn't ignore. He had a bed waiting for him in sober living. The arrangements were made.

We had a plan. He was now going back on what we planned.

"I don't need all that," he said. "I can handle it on my own."

Those words sent a chill down my spine. I'd heard them before. I knew what they really meant: "I'm not ready."

And I couldn't stay to watch the unraveling again.

During the time he was in rehab, I was making arrangements to put whatever remaining furniture and items that I wasn't able to sell or give away in storage. This is when his sister even offered to help me pack his stuff and bring totes and boxes. All of his important paperwork and storage key would be given to his father for safe keeping. He would know how and where to make payments. I wanted to make sure that when he was ready to get a place of his own or whatever he was going to do, he would have some items and the stuff wouldn't just go to waste. Like I previously mentioned, I will meet someone halfway as long as they are putting in the effort and doing their part.

It broke my heart to know that he was reneging on the plan. At that time, that was additional confirmation that we were done and closure that I needed. I stopped packing and canceled the storage arrangements. I continued with my efforts to sell MY remaining items and furniture. At this point, I didn't have the energy to manage someone else's life anymore. Especially someone who didn't want the help.

When he got out of rehab, I stayed another month or so and continued working and doing my own thing. I stayed partly out of guilt and partly from compassion. I didn't want him to get out and be alone without any positivity around him or a support system. Even though he decided not to go to sober living, he was still motivated to remain sober. He went to the outpatient center and got on medication-assisted treatment, including the monthly shot that would make him physically sick if he drank. I took him to appointments, helped him get back on his feet. I played the supportive role, like I always had. But this time, I didn't do it out of hope for us—I did it for closure. For peace.

His next focus was getting his car back. It became an obsession. With some help from family, he retrieved it. But with the car came the return of old behaviors. The illusion of progress shattered. He missed his next shot. The excuses returned like clockwork. It was happening all over again.

And I was done.

The final straw wasn't a big blowout. It wasn't a dramatic revelation. It was the quiet realization that he simply wasn't willing to do the work. I had spent years trying to hold us both together and now I was choosing to hold only myself.

My return trip home came sooner than expected. I started preparing to leave. There was nothing left for me there. I didn't tell him at first. I didn't know the exact date and didn't have all the details figured out yet. I wanted to wait until I had definitive plans and had to yet again, make sure I was safe.

While I was getting things in order, I was still working with notary clients and accepting roles in productions. I was offered the opportunity to play a flight attendant on the season finale of Chicago Med. A spark was reignited in me. Dressed in the uniform, standing in the mock cabin, pretending to smile as passengers boarded—it felt real. It felt like me stepping into the life I had always wanted, if only for a scene.

The experience awakened something in me. A sense of agency. A whisper that said, "You can still become her—the woman you dreamed of being before all this."

Being a Flight Attendant had danced around the edges of my life for years. My father worked for a major airline growing up. Flying has always been in my blood. As a child, we'd board flights with a sense of excitement and pride, my dad's employee status giving us extra care. The flight crew always looked after us. Even the gate agents smiled when they saw his name. It made me feel special—like I belonged to a world of status and prestige.

What did I have to lose? What else did I have going on? I got excited and looked at this as a sign to take it for real. "This could be your fresh start and clean slate. The segway to your new life and the life you've dreamed about as a child."

So, I applied.

Not just to one airline. I applied everywhere. Regional carriers. Major airlines. I scoured job boards. Filled out endless applications. And when the invitations for interviews started rolling in, I didn't hesitate. There was no looking back now. I THEN shared with him my plans. I still had a few weeks left, but now that I had solid and confirmed dates for interviews, backing out and changing my mind was not an option. I did that on purpose. Holding myself accountable and putting an end date on my stay, no matter what.

When it was time for me to leave, I packed the car—again— my now ritualistic escape route. A trunk full of the items I brought and any additional things I didn't want to leave behind this time. There was not going to be another time. I wasn't able to sell and get rid of everything I wanted to but I was ok with that. I was ok with walking away for the final time and leaving the rest of my old life behind. Physically. It wasn't just about leaving the city. It was about leaving the story we'd written together. A story that had dragged me through highs and lows, love and loss, hope and heartbreak. I was exhausted from trying to co-author a narrative that he had long stopped contributing to with sincerity.

Goodbye

Goodbye is not bitter.
It's a soft exhale after holding my breath for too long.
It's a closing door that no longer aches—
just a gentle click,
and quiet peace on the other side.

I've outgrown the version of me
who kept trying to make broken things bloom.
Who mistook pain for purpose
and silence for safety.

I used to beg for closure,
now I understand—
peace is the closure.
Distance is the answer.
And letting go is the lesson.

You were a chapter, not the whole book.
And now, I'm writing again—
with softer hands,
clearer eyes,
and a heart that finally beats for me.

So, goodbye.
Not with anger,
but with gratitude.
For the pain that taught me power,
for the ending that became my beginning.

Chapter 9

Stepping into My Becoming

"Discernment is the ability to accurately assess opportunities, people and situations by separating signal from noise and intention from presentation. It involves evaluating alignment, risk and impact rather than potential, pressure or appearance. Discernment guides decisions based on clarity, experience and self-trust, ensuring engagement only where safety, integrity and sustainability are present."

The ride home seemed to go by quickly. I was eager to get back home so I could start the interview process. I planned my departure so that as soon as I got home, I was turning right back around the next day to fly out for my first interview. Within the first month that I returned home I had 5 interviews lined up. Some were virtual and others were face to face. I ended up receiving three solid job offers. I was excited that I had options. I had to do a little more research before I accepted my final offer and received my training date. There was a lot I had to take into consideration. Becoming a Flight Attendant isn't just something you wake up one day and decide this is something I'll try. It is a complete lifestyle adjustment and you have to evaluate if the lifestyle is for you. At that time in my life, I didn't have anything else significant going on. I felt this would be the perfect opportunity to fulfill one of my childhood dreams and get the clean slate and fresh start I was looking for. I ended up accepting 2 of the jobs...one was for a regional airline and one was for a charter airline with a lot of lengthy international flying. I accepted both because I still was undecided as they were 2 completely different opportunities that would provide completely different experiences. The regional opportunity would be shorter flights, domestic flying, smaller work environment as well as smaller planes. The charter opportunity would provide the opportunity to travel weeks at a time to beautiful international locations. However, this would include longer flights, larger crews, larger planes and more passengers. Then I had to consider the pay and overall benefits and which opportunity would best align with what I wanted to experience and what my life would look like. Even though I did accept both opportunities, I was leaning more to the Regional opportunity. I had secured training dates for both but the regional one was before the other. I made sure I had all my affairs in order and made the final decision to go all in with the regional opportunity and rescind the charter offer. I was excited and prepared to finally leave for training. I was able to take about eight months to focus on myself and rebuild my confidence and self worth. I did have a little anxiety kick in due to this being a new opportunity and I was stepping into the unknown and unfamiliar. But I was ready. What did I have to lose?

I had about a month left before I officially left for training. During that time, I picked up a part-time job working overnight at FEDEX. It was familiar. During college I worked at one of their locations in my college town of Jonesboro, Arkansas. I would help load the driver's trucks and also would work in the office from time to time completing paperwork for the drivers after they returned from their routes. It was very flexible and worked around my school schedule. Upon graduating, I secured an internship back home with FEDEX working in their IT department at their headquarters. I felt honored and took pride that I had that amazing opportunity. My internship ended at a time when they were going through a complete restructuring of the company and unfortunately, I did not get a position within their IT department. I did however end up working in their sort operations. Now over twenty years later I was right back in the same environment. FEDEX was actually a very good part-time opportunity. Full-time benefits, tuition reimbursement and the opportunity to grow rapidly within the company. It was a hard and physically demanding job but I was up for the challenge.

During the day, I'd fall into bed exhausted—mentally, physically, emotionally. I still continued to work toward my healing. I journaled about my fears, lit candles, listened to meditative music and pulled cards from my healing decks. I whispered prayers of gratitude, even on the days when everything felt heavy. Especially on those days.

I knew this next chapter wasn't going to be easy. But it was mine.

I still had flashbacks of the life I left but I knew there was so much more waiting for me on the other side. Even though I still hadn't completely detached, I finally stopped asking, "What do I need to do to make him better?" And started asking, "What do I need to do to become whole again?"

Becoming Whole Again

*There comes a time
when silence stops feeling empty
and starts feeling like peace.*

*When you no longer chase healing—
you embody it.*

*You stop trying to fix the past,
and start tending to the present.*

*You forgive yourself
for the ways you survived.
You honor the woman
who kept showing up
even when she didn't know how.*

*And one day, without forcing,
without fighting—
you realize you're no longer breaking.*

You're becoming.

*Whole.
Grounded.
Ready.*

*Not to escape—
but to arrive.*

Chapter 10

Leaving to Live

"Self-love is the practice of being present with yourself and allowing your life to be lived fully and honestly. It is choosing care over criticism, rest over depletion and moments of joy without guilt. Self-love means listening to what you need, honoring your limits and giving yourself permission to enjoy who you are and the life you are creating."

And just like that, I was off. Leaving for flight attendant training was more than a dream come true—it was a release. A deep breath after years of holding everything in. It was me finally turning the page, walking into a new chapter that didn't begin with heartbreak or chaos. For the first time in what felt like forever, I was choosing something purely for me.

I needed to get out of my parents' house—not just physically, but energetically. I needed space from the watchful eyes, the subtle judgment, the quiet reminders of what hadn't worked out. I needed distance from the versions of me that still echoed in those walls. I needed a clean slate. And for once, I wasn't running from something—I was running toward it.

Not knowing how to pack light, I brought everything I thought I could possibly need for 31 days: clothes, my complete bathroom, books, vitamins, even "Baby Girl." When I arrived in Salt Lake City, I was nervous but excited. The training was intense—long hours, strict protocols, drills, tests—but I thrived under the pressure. It reminded me that I was capable. That I could focus, excel and adapt. Each day I spent in that training center was another day further away from the chaos I had left behind.

We were broken up into groups—A, B, C and D—each with different schedules, rotating days off and random class times to mimic the unpredictability of real flight schedules. Some mornings began before the sun; some nights we didn't sleep at all. It was physically exhausting, mentally demanding and emotionally revealing. But it was also exhilarating. There were rules for everything—what to wear, how to speak, what to carry. If you didn't have your passport or flashlight, you went home. If you failed more than one test, you went home. People left on the first day. The expectations were clear: show up sharp, stay ready or leave.

I studied harder than I had in years. There were four airline partners—Delta, United, American and Alaska—each with their own procedures, standards and aircraft configurations. I learned how to evacuate a plane, administer CPR, de-escalate angry passengers and stay calm when everything around me felt chaotic. Our group bonded through pressure. We turned hotel patios into mock planes, sticking Post-its on chairs to simulate cabin rows. We practiced drills in parking lots, studied while eating barbecue and sipping on a cocktail and leaned on each other when the exhaustion hit. It was beautiful chaos—and it reminded me just how strong I was.

When we finally graduated, the pride I felt wasn't just about earning wings. It was about what those wings represented: perseverance, transformation, rebirth.

Meanwhile, back in Chicago, things continued to unravel. Though I had tried to cut off communication, we still spoke occasionally. He was struggling, as I expected. His support system had crumbled. Friends disappeared. Family offered just enough to say they'd tried. He was left to face himself—and he didn't like what he saw.

Meanwhile, I was thriving. I was becoming the woman I had once only imagined—confident, free, whole. I made new friends, ate lunch with other trainees, swapped stories about travel dreams and future layovers. I belonged in that space—and for the first time in a long time, I didn't feel like I had to shrink to fit in. I was expanding.

I was no longer living in reaction to trauma. I was no longer tethered to someone else's potential. I was no longer shrinking to fit into a love that barely made room for me. Still, healing isn't linear. There were days I missed him—not for who he was, but for who I had hoped he'd become. I grieved the loss of potential. I mourned the future we had once planned. And sometimes, in quiet moments, I wondered if I'd given up too soon.

But then I'd remember the bathroom floor. The slurred insults. The silent suffering. The loneliness of lying next to someone who couldn't see me. And I'd remember that leaving wasn't betrayal—it was salvation.

During one of our last conversations, he accused me of abandoning him. Said I "ran home to my parents" like a coward. That I gave up when things got hard. I didn't argue. I let him say what he needed to say. Because I had learned something crucial: I didn't need to defend my decision to someone who never protected my heart. I had done the work. I had stayed longer than I should have. I had loved harder than I'd been loved in return. And now, I was done explaining my liberation to the person who imprisoned me.

As the weeks passed, I continued to grow. Training ended. I passed—with flying colors. I received my base assignment, my wings and the start date for my new life. I returned home briefly—just long enough to gather the rest of my things, hug my parents and say goodbye. This time, not to escape something, but to embrace something new.

And something beautiful happened in the months that followed. I began to fall in love with myself. Not in a superficial way. Not in a "treat yourself" way. But in the deepest, most sacred way possible. I started honoring my boundaries. Celebrating my accomplishments. Being gentle with my imperfections. I stopped negotiating my worth. I started protecting my peace with the same fierceness I once used to protect his potential.

I traveled. I made new memories. I built a new life. And slowly, the detachment became complete. No more phone calls. No more hope. No more waiting.

I wasn't stuck anymore. I wasn't between a rock and a hard place. I climbed out.

And for the first time in a very long time... I was free.

Rise Above It All

When you notice the air tastes different—
not because the world has changed,
but because you have.
The weight you carried
no longer fits your hands.
The rooms that once knew your silence
can no longer hold your song.
You start to see beauty
in the places that once held pain.
You start to thank the storms
for what they washed away.
You stop waiting to be rescued and realize—
you already saved yourself.
Healing was never about going back.
It was about coming home.
You no longer chase love
that asks you to shrink.
You no longer apologize
for needing peace.
You no longer explain
why you chose yourself.
You rise quietly,
not to prove a point—
but because your spirit
finally remembers how to breathe.
This is what freedom feels like.
Soft.
Steady.
Sacred.
Yours.

Chapter 11

A New City, A New Self

"Purging is the gentle act of letting go of what has grown heavy or no longer fits—old thoughts, habits, emotions and energy carried from earlier seasons of life. It is a compassionate clearing that allows space for rest, clarity and renewal. Purging supports growth by honoring what has been outgrown and welcoming what is ready to emerge."

After training, I relocated to Denver. I didn't know anyone there—and that was exactly the point. I needed a clean slate. A place untouched by my past. A city where no one looked at me and saw the pain I'd carried, where no one expected explanations or apologies.

I found a room to rent through a Facebook group for flight attendants. At first, I scrolled past the post, thinking nothing of it. But it kept reappearing, almost like it was calling me. When I finally reached out, the woman on the other end felt like an instant connection—same airline, similar energy, kind eyes.

Within days, I had a place to call home.

Denver was unlike any place I had lived before. The air was crisp, the sky impossibly blue and the mountains stood like ancient guardians at the edge of the city. There was a kind of silence there—not empty, but peaceful.

A silence that lets you hear your own thoughts again.

It wasn't a big city and that was a blessing. I'd always had a quiet kind of soul—social, but not loud. Crowds made me anxious; noise made me retreat.

In Denver, there was stillness.

Space.

Grace.

The energy was softer, slower. It let me breathe in a way I hadn't realized I'd been holding back for years.

For the first time in a long time, I felt invisible—in the best way. No one there knew my story. I could walk through the streets without the shadow of my past trailing behind me. I didn't have to explain the heartbreak, the loss, the rebuilding. I could simply exist. Introduce myself as who I was *now*, not who I had been.

That freedom was healing.

Denver wasn't just a location change—it was a soul recalibration. I started waking up earlier, not out of obligation, but because I wanted to. I'd open the blinds and let the sunlight spill across my face. I made coffee slowly, savoring the ritual instead of rushing through it.

I began to recognize the feeling of calm in my body— something I hadn't felt in years.

For the first time, there was no heavy silence in the next room.

No unpredictable mood shifts.

No need to brace myself before speaking.

Just peace.

Me.

Sunlight.

Possibility.

I started taking care of myself again—genuinely, intentionally. I got back into skincare, journaling, stretching and sitting in quiet reflection. I played soft music, lit candles and listened to my breath. I watched the mountains from my window and realized they mirrored my own strength— grounded, still, unshakable, no matter the storm.

I didn't own much and strangely, that made me feel free. Everything I needed fit into a few suitcases and a storage unit back home. At first, that reality stung—it made me feel like I had lost so much. But with time, I realized it was a kind of liberation.

I wasn't weighed down by things that no longer served me.

Every time I visited home, I'd take something new from storage—and let something go. Clothes that no longer reflected who I was becoming. Old notebooks filled with pain and survival. Gifts from people who had betrayed my trust. I released them all. Each time I did, I felt lighter—as though I was shedding layers of my old self to make room for the woman I was becoming.

I started exploring again. I hiked trails lined with wildflowers, wandered through local markets, took myself on quiet dates and learned to enjoy my own company. Sometimes I'd spend hours in a café with a book, just existing. Watching life unfold around me.

Feeling safe in my own skin again.

I met new people—not many, but the right ones. Other flight attendants, creatives, kind souls who didn't need to know my past to accept my presence. We shared stories over drinks, talked about places we wanted to visit, laughed about life between flights. Some of us had nothing in common except the desire to start over—and that was enough.

Little by little, I started reconnecting with my creativity.

And through it all, I realized something unexpected—being a flight attendant wasn't just a job. It was part of my healing.

People board planes carrying invisible baggage—joy, grief, fear, exhaustion, hope. I began to see how a small act—a smile, a kind word, a warm gesture—could change someone's entire experience. I wasn't just serving drinks or giving safety demos. I was holding space.

That was something I had always done—even when I couldn't name it. Now, I was doing it thirty thousand feet above the ground and it felt sacred.

I calmed children flying alone, offered tissues to women quietly crying in window seats and handed water to men too proud to ask. I listened to elderly passengers share memories of lost loves and long lives. Each act reminded me of what I once needed most—someone to see me, to make me feel safe.

And now, I was becoming that person for others.

This wasn't just a job. It was a mission. A ministry of quiet compassion.

It was healing—in motion.

The Art of Starting Over

*There is a tenderness
in beginning again—
a softness that comes
when the storm inside you
finally quiets.*

*Starting over isn't forgetting.
It's remembering yourself differently—
without the ache,
without the apology,
without the weight of proving
that you were worth saving.*

*It's walking into rooms
you once feared,
and breathing easy.
It's hearing your name
and not flinching.
It's realizing the world
didn't fall apart when you chose peace.*

*Starting over is sacred.
It's the whisper of sunlight
through an open window,
the stillness between heartbeats
when you realize
you made it out.*

*It's no longer chasing the fire—
but learning to be the warmth.*

So you unpack slowly.
You laugh louder.
You let the quiet mornings hold you.
You trust the unfolding.

And you finally see—
starting over was never the ending.

It was just the beginning.

Chapter 12

Reclaiming Old Dreams

"Passion is the refusal to abandon what has called to you since the beginning. It is a childhood desire hardened by discipline and proven through consistency, repetition and execution. Passion is not emotion or inspiration—it is commitment sustained through doubt, failure and fatigue until mastery is earned."

As I settled nicely into my new life, my old passions quietly tapped me on the shoulder—reminding me they had never left. They were simply waiting for me to return. I hadn't abandoned them; I had just been trying to survive. When I finally found clarity, stability and peace, I realized I could create again—not from pressure, but from joy. Not because I had to, but because I finally got to.

The first passion that rose back to the surface was my love for modeling and acting.

I've dreamed of being an actress for as long as I can remember. Even as a shy little girl, something in me wanted to be seen, celebrated and expressive. People often assume children crave attention, but I never wanted attention—I wanted expression. I wanted to tell stories, bring characters to life, feel alive through creativity and presence. Before I ever stood in front of a camera, I was just a sensitive, intuitive, imaginative child trying to understand herself. I wanted to be seen—not for performance, but for authenticity. Modeling and acting became the first places where my inner world made sense.

My first photoshoot was when I was around eight or nine. My mom dusted a little translucent powder on my face, dabbed a soft lipstick across my lips and sent me into a black-and-white shoot that would imprint itself on my memory forever. I still remember the photographer gently adjusting my shoulders and saying, "Roll them back." My smile was awkward, but the moment the camera clicked, something unlocked inside me. It didn't feel foreign. It felt familiar. Like home.

That spark never left.

My parents did what they could to support my dreams. My mom took me to my first audition—for *Life with Mikey*. I didn't get the role, but I was mesmerized by the process. Even the uncomfortable parts couldn't dim the excitement I felt simply being in that world. Something in me knew I belonged there.

As I got older, I invested in myself. At sixteen, I worked at Burlington Coat Factory and used every paycheck for clothes, shoes and modeling classes. I enrolled in a six-month program that taught me posing, runway, speech and presence. I leaned toward modeling because it allowed me to express myself without speaking; my shyness was still a wall I didn't know how to climb. My mom used to tell me, "Wendy, you're scared to hear your own voice," and she wasn't wrong.

I joined an urban modeling troupe in Memphis and started doing trade shows, bridal expos, TV segments and more. I even had a recurring role on an ABC 24 youth show called *We Are Tomorrow, R You?* as "Wendy Word," teaching vocabulary and acting out scenes with "Wally Word." It was playful, empowering and my first real taste of production life.

Life shifted again.
I went to college.
I paused.
But the passion stayed awake inside me.

A two-week family visit to Chicago turned into a twenty-year chapter of my life. And once I found my ground, I returned to modeling. Chicago molded me, sharpened me, expanded me. I became known for my runway walk—a fusion of my formal training, my urban flair and my own personality. I loved everything about that world: the community, the creativity, the long hours on set, the energy, the people who would become lifelong friends.

I worked with major brands, talented photographers and powerful creative teams. I also stepped into extra and background acting for well-known TV shows and films shooting in Chicago. That work gave me real set experience, behind-the-scenes insight, professionalism and an understanding of presence. I was often chosen for specialty or director-selected moments. Sometimes I had my own trailer, stylist, hair and makeup artist and crew catering. For a girl who had once been painfully shy, those moments meant something.

But the industry is a double-edged sword.
It celebrates you and breaks you at the same time.

I battled body image, fluctuating weight, feeling not good enough, perfectionism, rejection and pressure. The eating disorder I didn't admit I had until age forty-four had its roots in those early years. I watched my parents diet growing up and internalized restriction as normal. I began the Atkins Diet young, eating mainly meat, using laxatives, believing thinness equaled success. And when a runway instructor told me, "You look good—keep doing what you're doing," it hooked me deeper. I received the praise I associated with belonging, so I kept going—even when it wasn't healthy.

Despite the internal battles, I excelled. I booked work at all sizes—plus, straight, signed, unsigned, freelance, barter, paid. I hustled. I reinvented. I survived.

And then came the moment that changed everything:

"The Lady in the Blue Dress."

A moment I never planned or expected. That appearance on *The Steve Harvey Show* became bigger than anything I had ever intentionally pursued. It went viral. The world saw me before I fully saw myself. They didn't see the shy little girl. They didn't see the broken parts. They didn't see the woman healing quietly inside.

They saw confidence.
They saw presence.
They saw beauty.
They saw "The Lady in the Blue Dress."

The recognition came with love and hate—praise and cruelty. People uplifted me while others body-shamed, mocked and criticized. I felt exposed, adored, judged and celebrated all at once. I was recognized everywhere—online, in person, on the street. It was surreal. It was overwhelming. It was everything I had once dreamed of...and yet nothing like I imagined.

And then life shifted again.

I felt the pull to see what else was possible. I told myself I would move to Atlanta or LA and restart my career. After several trips and research, I chose LA. I moved January 1, 2015. I sublet rooms off Craigslist while working a contract mortgage auditing job, booked agencies and started acting and modeling again. I shipped my car. I recreated myself. I felt like I was expanding into my next chapter.

Then everything back home fell apart.

My tenants spiraled into a nightmare situation. I had two choices: stay in LA and manage chaos from across the country or return to Chicago and fix it myself. I chose responsibility, even though it broke my heart. I returned. I felt disappointed. I felt like a failure. But I knew I had made the right decision.

Back in Chicago, my life slowly unraveled. I used modeling and acting to cope, to escape, to survive. Eventually, I reached the breaking point. I walked away from everything I knew and went to my parents' home for a reset—a real reset. Healing. Silence. Recovery. Rebuilding. I stayed for ~8 months.

And when I finally felt ready, I moved to Denver to embark on a new journey.

Starting over in Denver brought me back to myself. When I was ready, I submitted to agencies and signed quickly. I still had one agent in Chicago, so I flew back and forth for work—including a United Airlines campaign. It felt good to return to the industry, but this time on my own terms. One of the reasons I eventually became a flight attendant was to support my acting and modeling career—to be able to travel for castings and gigs without limits.

When one agency relationship ended, I returned to another agency that had originally wanted to sign me earlier. That led me to one of the biggest and most respected agencies in Denver. With representation secured, I continued rebuilding—not through chaos or coping, but through clarity and alignment. And for the first time in a very long time, I began returning to myself—not through hustle, not through running and not through survival, but through alignment.

I wasn't chasing roles anymore.
I wasn't trying to prove anything to anyone—including myself. I wasn't using work to escape or numb.

This time was different.

I was rebuilding slowly... intentionally... and on my own terms.

Every part of my identity that I picked back up—modeling, acting, traveling, reconnecting with my creative expression— I chose it with clarity, with wisdom and with love. I wasn't forcing opportunities. I wasn't shrinking myself to fit an industry standard. I wasn't breaking myself to belong.

I was coming home—to my voice, my body, my dreams and my truth.

Denver wasn't the beginning of a new life.
It was the beginning of the **real** me.

The woman who finally knew her worth.
The woman who no longer abandoned herself for acceptance.
The woman who could return to modeling—not from pressure or survival, but from grounded confidence and genuine joy.

Slow.
Steady.
Aligned.
Unrushed, unbothered, unbroken.

This was the version of me who was ready to rise again— not as the girl who survived everything... but as the woman who was finally ready to live.

Unrushed, Unbothered, Unbroken

I am rebuilding gently now—
not rushing, not chasing,
not proving anything to anyone.

I'm reintroducing my passions
one sacred piece at a time,
with intention, with clarity,
with a steady heart.

No more forcing.
No more survival.
No more measuring my worth
by how fast something happens

I am creating from peace now—
from joy, from purpose,
from a love that finally includes me.

What comes next,
I choose on my own terms.
What grows next,
grows with grace.

My life is no longer something
I'm trying to catch up to.
It's something I'm finally
able to walk into—
softly, fully,
and whole.

Chapter 13

The Rise and Fall

"An entrepreneur is someone who keeps building after losses, chooses discipline over excuses and refuses to stop when progress is slow, lonely or unforgiving. Entrepreneurship is the repeated act of standing back up, correcting course and executing with greater precision after every setback. It is earned through pressure, failure and persistence and sustained by the refusal to quit when quitting would be easier. An entrepreneur rises not because the path is kind, but because walking away is not an option."

It feels refreshing when you can finally look back at your life with clear eyes and recognize just how far you've come. I would've never imagined this would be my story—especially not unfolding in Denver. I had big plans. I was supposed to be a millionaire by thirty, with a multi-million-dollar real estate portfolio, multiple businesses and my face on major retail and beauty campaigns. That was the vision. That was the plan. And honestly? It felt reachable.

Entrepreneurship isn't new to me. I've been an entrepreneur since childhood—selling stickers, greeting cards, cookies, candy, modeling, acting... I was always creating something, always figuring out how to build from nothing. Growing up, my dreams were simple but bold: be a flight attendant, be a model and be an entrepreneur. As I began healing and rebuilding my life years later, I realized I had already checked two off that list. Now it was time to reintroduce the third one back into my life.

I watched both of my parents go in and out of different business ventures and multi-level marketing companies when I was younger. I joined them sometimes—not for the sales, because I've never been the pushy sales type. What I loved were the leadership trainings, the motivational books, the CDs, the personal development mindset. The products were cool, but my soul was there for the growth. Looking back, I now understand exactly where my entrepreneurial fire came from. I was never meant to work for someone forever. Even as a child, I knew I wanted something of my own. I didn't know what it would be yet, but I knew it would belong to me.

After college, I moved back home to Memphis. I had a summer internship lined up, but I still needed to figure out my next step. Around that same time, my mom unexpectedly became a notary because of a tragedy—my uncle passed away suddenly in New Jersey and she had to travel to retrieve my aunt who had Alzheimer's. That whole situation pushed her into entrepreneurship and watching her rebuild herself lit a spark in me.

So I followed her guidance and got my notary commission. At first, I helped her with her business, shadowing her, learning the ropes and getting comfortable. Once I found my rhythm, I branched out on my own. We became a little tag-team—sharing clients, supporting each other, building something from nothing.

My first official business started with the bare basics— a $50 printer, a ream of legal and letter paper, an extra toner cartridge, my computer and a few office supplies. That was it. But I worked with what I had and it was enough.

As business grew, I reinvested everything. Better equipment. Better tools. Better marketing. Before long, I had built a strong reputation and had a roster of solid, reputable clients. But eventually, I wanted more. There wasn't anything left for me in Memphis. I needed a bigger arena—so I moved to Chicago.

I started out working in the IT field there and once I got settled, I relaunched my mobile notary business in a major city full of opportunity. I began part-time, but business grew fast—so fast that my part-time income surpassed my full-time salary. I didn't jump impulsively. I transitioned responsibly. I tracked my income for months, confirmed steady work with my regular clients and made sure the demand could sustain me long-term. When everything aligned, I resigned and went full-time into entrepreneurship.

And then came the subprime lending era—when anyone could get a loan.

No documentation.
No real verification.
Just decent credit and a signature.

Because of that, the real estate and lending industries were booming—and so was the notary business. I was easily doing four to five closings a day, back-to-back... on location, at lenders' offices, title companies, homes, boardrooms... everywhere. Money was everywhere. Opportunity was everywhere. I was young, making good money and yeah—I was starting to feel myself a bit. I already owned my first condo, I was leveling up and I wanted to invest. I wanted to grow.

That's when my real estate chapter truly began.

All the leadership material I was consuming started shaping my mindset—Robert Kiyosaki, Rich Dad Poor Dad, the Cash Flow Quadrant... all of it. I didn't know everything, but I knew enough from the closings I had been performing— seeing the numbers, reviewing documents, talking with clients—and with a long-time friend in the business guiding me, I decided to step into real estate investing.

Chicago at the time was also in the running to host the Olympics. And the entire city was buzzing with "The Olympics are coming! The Olympics are coming!" That was the pitch everywhere. Everyone was saying it was the perfect time to invest—get in early, buy in the surrounding areas and get ready for the boom. The areas around the proposed sites were labeled "up-and-coming," and on paper, it looked like a perfect strategy. Or so I thought.

I was introduced to an investment group through a co-worker and friend. I trusted her, so I didn't have any reason to think she'd steer me wrong. But she did—unintentionally or not. When I met with them, they painted the perfect picture: they'd help build my portfolio, assist with income generation, handle renovations… the whole nine. They showed me several properties and I selected two as a bundled deal. I was still green, still independent, wanting to prove myself as an adult. Looking back, that was definitely a moment where I should have asked for more help.

I hired an attorney, used their preferred lender and let their team handle the renovations because the properties were still being finished. Everything moved quickly and it felt like everything was falling into place. When it was time to close, I was out of town visiting my parents. They sent a car service to pick me up from the airport. I was ready. I was purchasing two properties—a luxury 3-bedroom, 3-bath condo and a 3-flat building. My plan was to rent them both out while keeping my condo in the suburbs as my primary home.

The closings went smooth. I felt proud. I felt grown. I felt like I was exactly where I was supposed to be.

But things unraveled quickly.

The condo I moved into started looking more appealing than my place in the suburbs, so I rented my original condo to my cousin and moved into the city. I rented out the entire building and for a moment everything looked aligned. Until it wasn't.

Everything started going wrong at once.

The building had plumbing disasters.
Roofing issues.
Water heaters leaking carbon monoxide.
Furnaces malfunctioning.
Flooding.
Repairs that never stayed repaired.

Meanwhile, my condo in the 6-unit building exploded into its own chaos. They turned the association over to us, the owners—six strangers responsible for everything. I was somehow elected president. We still had warranties, but the developers were shady, aggressive, sending unskilled workers, threatening us when we pushed back. We filed complaints with every agency—building department, attorney general, state's attorney, consumer affairs. Inspectors were coming out daily. I was going to court constantly. Eventually, the building department lawyers told me I didn't need to keep attending— they had it under control.

It kept getting worse. The basement unit flooded repeatedly. Owners were miserable. We were all filing separate complaints. And then we found out the developers were ex-drug dealers running a mortgage fraud ring with real estate agents, mortgage brokers, lenders, title companies and even prominent attorneys in their pocket.

Everything made sense.

By that point I had refinanced my original condo to pull money out and try to save everything… and that put me in a bind. I eventually lost everything—every property. I handed the 3-flat back with a deed-in-lieu of foreclosure. I walked away from the condo. Eventually, I lost the one in the suburbs too. I filed bankruptcy for a clean start.

Then the FBI and state's attorney contacted me. They wanted me to come in for questioning because the entire organization had been under investigation. They showed me documents with my signature that I had never seen before—loan docs, disclosures... forged paperwork. They were eventually indicted and sent to prison.

And in the middle of all of that, I did a closing for a judge who casually mentioned a big case involving mortgage fraud. When he said the attorney's name, my stomach dropped—it was one of the same men involved in the ring.

It gave me a strange mix of closure and disbelief.

I had lost everything and had to rebuild my life completely.

I found a one-bedroom apartment thanks to the maintenance man from my previous condo complex—someone I trusted like an uncle. He vouched for me. He helped me find my footing again. Ironically, years later he would become one of my biggest nightmares, but at that moment, he was a blessing.

I rebuilt. Again.

I picked up jobs when needed and continued my mobile notary business. I got into contract mortgage auditing and anti-money laundering investigations for financial institutions and the government. I was self-taught, but the years of loan closings made me sharp. With their training, I excelled. I loved it. I bought another condo. A new car. I returned to full-time entrepreneurship and became a landlord again.

When I moved to LA, I was juggling being a landlord, modeling, acting, contracting with financial institutions and preparing to restart my notary business in California. But then everything fell apart with my tenants back home and I had to return to Chicago to fix it. The plan was to sell and go back to LA—but life had other plans. It took over a year to sell. By the time it did, I had built an entire life again in Chicago—relationships, a new job, modeling, acting, rebuilding again.

That's when I stepped into credit repair. I met a man in the industry who became my mentor. I worked with him, learned formally this time and eventually branched out on my own. I established Savvy Financial Solutions. Business grew fast through word of mouth. Another business partner came along and we collaborated for a long while, each running our own businesses but working together.

Through all this, I had ups and downs, slow seasons and layoffs. I realized one thing about myself: I'm unemployable and not in a bad way—I just wasn't built to be controlled, mistreated or silenced. I have boundaries and a voice. And I always knew that if I had to grind harder, I would.

Life kept life-ing, but I always rebuilt. I always created. I always made a way.

When I moved again—my final move before my life collapsed—I was running a credit repair business, my notary business, modeling, acting and still taking contract AML work. My plate was full. Too full. But I kept adding more. I got an office to separate home from work. I started Turo to rent out my car. It did so well I bought another. Then another. I guided beginners through the process, helping them set up their profiles and get started.

I kept myself busy because behind closed doors my life was falling apart. My internal world was crumbling. Nothing was rooted in joy anymore—everything was survival. My spiritual business came next, The Sacred Soul Sister—a beautiful idea born from necessity, not alignment. I helped others the way I had helped myself. Business was good. But everything I was building was coming from a place of "I have to," not "I get to." I was running five different businesses on fumes.

And when you refuse to listen to the whispers, the universe sends the storm.

My office burning down was the beginning.

Slowly, everything inside me and around me was forcing me to wake up. I couldn't outrun it anymore. I couldn't distract myself with work anymore. My health was tanking. My mental state was deteriorating. My spirit was exhausted.

I had to save myself.

I had to choose myself.

I walked away from everything I thought I loved.
I walked away from everything I had strategically built.
I walked away from a life that was no longer serving me.

I didn't know what was next.
I didn't know how I would rebuild.
But I knew I had to leave—or I wouldn't survive.

And that was the beginning of the version of me writing this now.

But Still I Rise

*My journey hasn't been a straight line—
it's been a series of beginnings, setbacks, lessons and
rebirths.*

*I've built before.
I've lost things I thought would last.
I've had to start again when I didn't want to,
with nothing but faith and a vision only I could see.*

And still—I'm here.

*Not because it was easy.
Not because everything worked.
But because something in me refuses to give up.*

*Every setback made me wiser.
Every detour made me stronger.
Every restart made me more aligned and more intentional.*

I am not behind—I am evolving.

*This time, I'm building with clarity.
With courage.
With experience.
With purpose.*

*I trust myself.
I trust my mission.
And I know:*

My comeback is already unfolding.

Chapter 14

"An awakening or rebirth, is a forced shift in awareness that occurs when denial and survival mechanisms fail. It marks the collapse of previously tolerated realities and compels the dismantling of an outdated identity. A rebirth establishes new parameters for perception, boundaries and decision-making based on acknowledged truth. The change is irreversible."

So here we are. I am living my fab F.A.M.E Life™—the life I dreamed of as a child and finally created as a woman. What started as innocent childhood fantasies turned into my lived reality. I AM a Flight Attendant, a Model and an Entrepreneur.

The joy, peace, self-love, sunshine and confidence you see radiating from me did not come without a price. I've had a beautiful life—a happy childhood, a creative adolescence and an adulthood full of accomplishments, recognition and success. But I've also been through the trenches. And every time, I came out wiser, stronger, more aligned and more in tune with my purpose.

There were cycles where I lost everything and had to rebuild. Then lost everything again. And rebuilt again. But this last time? It hit different. Because this time... I didn't just lose things. I lost myself. And nothing else matters if you lose that.

You can always replace possessions. But when you break apart inside, you have to rebuild piece by piece—intentionally, slowly, without a roadmap, without a timeline and without anyone telling you how or when to heal. You have to listen to your body. Your heart. Your spirit. You have to give yourself grace. And most importantly—you have to forgive yourself.

People always say forgiveness is for you, not them. But let me be very clear... the only forgiveness I cared about was forgiving myself. Everyone else was optional. And I didn't need to wish anything bad on anyone who hurt me—life, karma and the universe handle that on their own.

My healing was intentional.
My healing was personal.
My healing was on purpose—every single day.

In 2019, I experienced one of the most intense and transformative awakenings of my life—something I didn't see coming and wasn't prepared for. Sure, I had gone through difficult seasons before, but this one was different. This was a full dismantling of everything I thought I knew about myself, my relationships, my life and my identity.

Some people call it a breakdown. But spiritually, it was a Dark Night of the Soul.

A Dark Night of the Soul is not sadness and it's not simply "going through a tough time." It is a spiritual unraveling—a deep inner purge where everything false, unhealthy, unhealed or misaligned gets exposed. It forces you to stop running, stop pretending, stop performing and truly face yourself—your wounds, patterns, fears, trauma, ego and truth. It is the collapse that initiates the rebirth. The breaking that makes room for becoming.

And that is exactly what happened to me.

My life was crumbling in front of my eyes. I felt helpless—watching the pieces fall apart with nothing left to hold onto except faith. At first, I slipped into a victim mindset, asking, "Why is this happening to me?" But eventually, I had to shift to, "Why is this happening for me?"

I prayed for clarity, protection, strength, wisdom and discernment. Slowly, painfully, the answers started coming. I saw my environment clearly. I saw the truth about my relationships. I saw the lies, distortions, patterns and illusions. My external world was shattering. My internal world was shattering. And in that moment, I learned—your outer world mirrors your inner world.

I began recognizing people for who they truly were — not for the version I wanted them to be. I saw how deeply I had abandoned myself. I saw how much I tolerated out of fear, loneliness and conditioning. I was stripped down to my core. Humbled. Exposed. But awakened.

Even though I was surrounded by people, I had no one. I retreated out of shame, embarrassment, guilt, resentment and pure confusion. The gossip behind my back was loud. I heard it. I felt it. But I was too exhausted to defend myself. And the worst part? The deepest betrayal came from someone under the same roof—someone destroying me from the inside out.

I justified his behavior. I explained away the abuse. But in reality...I was dying. I had to detach to save myself.

During that time, a friend introduced me to an online psychic reading app. What started as curiosity turned into desperation and eventually became a source of guidance. Some readings resonated, others didn't, but they led me toward greater spiritual understanding—soul contracts, karmic ties, ancestral cycles, intuitive gifts.

And eventually, I learned I was in a Twin Flame connection.

A Twin Flame connection is not romance or fairy dust—it is a spiritual mirror. A fire. A catalyst. It forces you to face the deepest parts of yourself: abandonment wounds, shadows, trauma, fears, patterns. It is not meant to comfort you; it is meant to awaken you. Twin Flames don't come into your life to complete you—they come to break you open so you can complete yourself.

That connection lit the match for my awakening.

I began researching, reading, listening and healing. I studied inner child work, shadow work, nervous system healing, reiki, energy clearing, intuition, trauma patterns—all of it. I dove headfirst into healing. I journaled for hours. I meditated. I cried. I unraveled. I masked.

If you didn't know my life was falling apart, you would've never guessed it. I didn't look like what I was going through. I didn't act like it either. I didn't let anyone close enough to see me break.

Everything I did—every tool I used—was originally just for me. My lifeline. My anchor.

Eventually, something shifted.
If these tools saved me, I realized I could help others with them too.

I started reading for others.
Helping others.
Supporting others.
Pouring into others.

But behind the scenes, my world was collapsing. I felt like a fraud—drowning while trying to help others swim.

I needed real help.
Professional help.
So I got into therapy and saw a psychiatrist.
Weekly sessions.
Medication.
Clarity.

That's when the truth came out:

I did NOT have Bipolar II.
I had PTSD.

I had C-PTSD.

And I had late diagnosed adult ADHD.

PTSD is trauma from specific events—a shock to the system.

C-PTSD is trauma from prolonged exposure to emotional, psychological or relational harm—trauma that reshapes your inner world and nervous system. And ADHD masked beneath trauma looks like chaos, overwhelm, shutdown, exhaustion, distraction—but it was really my nervous system trying to cope.

Understanding this brought relief.

It helped me understand myself with compassion instead of shame.

My therapist had me start a positivity journal—writing down everything I believed about myself, everything I loved about myself, everything I wanted to reclaim. Slowly, piece by piece, I rebuilt my self-worth.

But the final straw…the moment that snapped something in me forever… was the night he said, "Everybody thinks there's something spectacular about you, but there's nothing spectacular about you to me."

That was it.

That was the moment my soul said,

"Get up. It's time."

I stated my intentions.

I packed my things.

And left the day after Thanksgiving.

11/25/2022.

The day I reclaimed my life.

These last three years have been the hardest and the most beautiful of my entire journey.

I rebuilt myself.
I healed myself.
I returned to myself.
Piece by piece.
Truth by truth.
Day by day.

And the most unexpected twist?

Eleven Years later, the very moment people mocked me for—the blue dress, the elegance, the softness—became the moment that launched me into a new life.

The "Lady in the Blue Dress" became a movement. A symbol of healing, self-love, softness, joy and feminine power.

Millions embraced me—my energy, my story, my presence, my light.

The universe whispered,
"I told you this was yours."

I became a viral sensation all over again.
An icon.
Now a symbol of survival, transformation and rebirth.

The same moment that once brought ridicule...
now brings hope to millions.

I am still recognized everywhere—online and in real life.
I inspire people simply by being myself.
My light speaks before I do.
My story heals people without me even trying.

I had to lose everything—including myself—to become who I was always meant to be.

And now?
I am living my F.A.M.E Life™
Flight Attendant.
Model.
Entrepreneur.

The woman who healed on purpose—every single day.

Every tool I used to save myself, I now recreate so others can save themselves too.
Every lesson I learned becomes someone else's clarity.
Every wound I healed becomes someone else's roadmap.

I am the chosen one in my lineage.
The cycle breaker.
The healer.
The guide.

The woman who rose—intentionally, spiritually and unapologetically.

And I'm only getting started.

Thank you for holding space for my story—the messy parts, the real parts, the rising parts.

Sharing this journey hasn't always been easy, but I've learned that truth loses its weight when it's spoken—and sometimes, pieces of our story help someone else feel a little less alone.

My path hasn't been linear.
I've fallen.
I've rebuilt.
I've questioned everything—including myself.
But I kept going. And if you're reading this, something tells me you are, too.

If there is one message woven between these pages, it's this:

No matter how many times life knocks you down, you are capable of rising again—stronger, wiser and more aligned with who you're meant to be.

You are not alone.
You are not broken.
You are becoming.

Thank you for walking through this chapter with me.

— Wendy Nicole Davis

Healing on purpose everyday. Not because we have to, because we want to.

Healing On Purpose Everyday